C-147   CAREER EXAMINATION SERIES

This is your
PASSBOOK for...

Clerk-Typist

Test Preparation Study Guide
Questions & Answers

NATIONAL LEARNING CORPORATION®

COPYRIGHT NOTICE

This book is SOLELY intended for, is sold ONLY to, and its use is RESTRICTED to individual, bona fide applicants or candidates who qualify by virtue of having seriously filed applications for appropriate license, certificate, professional and/or promotional advancement, higher school matriculation, scholarship, or other legitimate requirements of education and/or governmental authorities.

This book is NOT intended for use, class instruction, tutoring, training, duplication, copying, reprinting, excerption, or adaptation, etc., by:

1) Other publishers
2) Proprietors and/or Instructors of "Coaching" and/or Preparatory Courses
3) Personnel and/or Training Divisions of commercial, industrial, and governmental organizations
4) Schools, colleges, or universities and/or their departments and staffs, including teachers and other personnel
5) Testing Agencies or Bureaus
6) Study groups which seek by the purchase of a single volume to copy and/or duplicate and/or adapt this material for use by the group as a whole without having purchased individual volumes for each of the members of the group
7) Et al.

Such persons would be in violation of appropriate Federal and State statutes.

PROVISION OF LICENSING AGREEMENTS – Recognized educational, commercial, industrial, and governmental institutions and organizations, and others legitimately engaged in educational pursuits, including training, testing, and measurement activities, may address request for a licensing agreement to the copyright owners, who will determine whether, and under what conditions, including fees and charges, the materials in this book may be used them. In other words, a licensing facility exists for the legitimate use of the material in this book on other than an individual basis. However, it is asseverated and affirmed here that the material in this book CANNOT be used without the receipt of the express permission of such a licensing agreement from the Publishers. Inquiries re licensing should be addressed to the company, attention rights and permissions department.

All rights reserved, including the right of reproduction in whole or in part, in any form or by any means, electronic or mechanical, including photocopying, recording, or by any information storage and retrieval system, without permission in writing from the Publisher.

Copyright © 2024 by
National Learning Corporation

212 Michael Drive, Syosset, NY 11791
(516) 921-8888 • www.passbooks.com
E-mail: info@passbooks.com

PUBLISHED IN THE UNITED STATES OF AMERICA

PASSBOOK® SERIES

THE *PASSBOOK® SERIES* has been created to prepare applicants and candidates for the ultimate academic battlefield – the examination room.

At some time in our lives, each and every one of us may be required to take an examination – for validation, matriculation, admission, qualification, registration, certification, or licensure.

Based on the assumption that every applicant or candidate has met the basic formal educational standards, has taken the required number of courses, and read the necessary texts, the *PASSBOOK® SERIES* furnishes the one special preparation which may assure passing with confidence, instead of failing with insecurity. Examination questions – together with answers – are furnished as the basic vehicle for study so that the mysteries of the examination and its compounding difficulties may be eliminated or diminished by a sure method.

This book is meant to help you pass your examination provided that you qualify and are serious in your objective.

The entire field is reviewed through the huge store of content information which is succinctly presented through a provocative and challenging approach – the question-and-answer method.

A climate of success is established by furnishing the correct answers at the end of each test.

You soon learn to recognize types of questions, forms of questions, and patterns of questioning. You may even begin to anticipate expected outcomes.

You perceive that many questions are repeated or adapted so that you can gain acute insights, which may enable you to score many sure points.

You learn how to confront new questions, or types of questions, and to attack them confidently and work out the correct answers.

You note objectives and emphases, and recognize pitfalls and dangers, so that you may make positive educational adjustments.

Moreover, you are kept fully informed in relation to new concepts, methods, practices, and directions in the field.

You discover that you are actually taking the examination all the time: you are preparing for the examination by "taking" an examination, not by reading extraneous and/or supererogatory textbooks.

In short, this PASSBOOK®, used directedly, should be an important factor in helping you to pass your test.

CLERK-TYPIST

DUTIES:
An employee in this class performs clerical and typing/word processing duties of limited difficulty and responsibility. The work of these positions, apart from typewriting, is similar in nature and level to that found in the clerk class. Duties of the position follow well-defined procedures and methods. Detailed instructions and close supervision are received at the beginning of work and on new assignments, but regular routine tasks are performed more independently and some initiative and judgment are utilized as experience is gained. The nature of the work is such that the employee may be required to operate a variety of office equipment. Employees may make arithmetical or other checks for accuracy of work performed by other employees, but they do not exercise direct supervision over other personnel. The work is performed under the direct supervision of assigned supervisory personnel, and is reviewed upon completion for content and accuracy. Does related work as required.

EXAMPLES OF WORK:
Types articles, forms, vendor's claims, letters, envelopes, memoranda, bulletins, reports, tabulations, purchase orders, cards, payrolls, trial calendar requisitions, marriage cards, copies of ordinances and resolutions, birth and death certificates and records, attendance and student records, case reports, commitment papers and other material using an alpha-numeric keyboard. Sorts and files correspondence; checks, vouchers, index cards or other materials, numerically, alphabetically or by other established classifications; sorts, dates stamps, distribute and/or deliver mail and packages; assists in the maintenance of personnel, payroll, equipment, or other records and in the preparation of reports; makes simple arithmetic calculations, computes data from requisitions, statistical reports, time reports or other records; occasionally may act as a receptionist and/or switchboard operator; operates standard office equipment including but not limited to photocopiers, fax machines, calculators, personal computers or computer terminals, and typewriters.

SUBJECTS OF THE EXAMINATION:
The written examination may test for knowledge, skills, and/or abilities in any of the following areas:
1. Spelling;
2. Alphabetizing;
3. Recordkeeping;
4. Clerical operations with letters and numbers;
5. Understanding and interpreting written material;
6. English usage; and
7. Proofreading.

HOW TO TAKE A TEST

I. YOU MUST PASS AN EXAMINATION

A. WHAT EVERY CANDIDATE SHOULD KNOW

Examination applicants often ask us for help in preparing for the written test. What can I study in advance? What kinds of questions will be asked? How will the test be given? How will the papers be graded?

As an applicant for a civil service examination, you may be wondering about some of these things. Our purpose here is to suggest effective methods of advance study and to describe civil service examinations.

Your chances for success on this examination can be increased if you know how to prepare. Those "pre-examination jitters" can be reduced if you know what to expect. You can even experience an adventure in good citizenship if you know why civil service exams are given.

B. WHY ARE CIVIL SERVICE EXAMINATIONS GIVEN?

Civil service examinations are important to you in two ways. As a citizen, you want public jobs filled by employees who know how to do their work. As a job seeker, you want a fair chance to compete for that job on an equal footing with other candidates. The best-known means of accomplishing this two-fold goal is the competitive examination.

Exams are widely publicized throughout the nation. They may be administered for jobs in federal, state, city, municipal, town or village governments or agencies.

Any citizen may apply, with some limitations, such as the age or residence of applicants. Your experience and education may be reviewed to see whether you meet the requirements for the particular examination. When these requirements exist, they are reasonable and applied consistently to all applicants. Thus, a competitive examination may cause you some uneasiness now, but it is your privilege and safeguard.

C. HOW ARE CIVIL SERVICE EXAMS DEVELOPED?

Examinations are carefully written by trained technicians who are specialists in the field known as "psychological measurement," in consultation with recognized authorities in the field of work that the test will cover. These experts recommend the subject matter areas or skills to be tested; only those knowledges or skills important to your success on the job are included. The most reliable books and source materials available are used as references. Together, the experts and technicians judge the difficulty level of the questions.

Test technicians know how to phrase questions so that the problem is clearly stated. Their ethics do not permit "trick" or "catch" questions. Questions may have been tried out on sample groups, or subjected to statistical analysis, to determine their usefulness.

Written tests are often used in combination with performance tests, ratings of training and experience, and oral interviews. All of these measures combine to form the best-known means of finding the right person for the right job.

II. HOW TO PASS THE WRITTEN TEST

A. NATURE OF THE EXAMINATION

To prepare intelligently for civil service examinations, you should know how they differ from school examinations you have taken. In school you were assigned certain definite pages to read or subjects to cover. The examination questions were quite detailed and usually emphasized memory. Civil service exams, on the other hand, try to discover your present ability to perform the duties of a position, plus your potentiality to learn these duties. In other words, a civil service exam attempts to predict how successful you will be. Questions cover such a broad area that they cannot be as minute and detailed as school exam questions.

In the public service similar kinds of work, or positions, are grouped together in one "class." This process is known as *position-classification*. All the positions in a class are paid according to the salary range for that class. One class title covers all of these positions, and they are all tested by the same examination.

B. FOUR BASIC STEPS

1) Study the announcement

How, then, can you know what subjects to study? Our best answer is: "Learn as much as possible about the class of positions for which you've applied." The exam will test the knowledge, skills and abilities needed to do the work.

Your most valuable source of information about the position you want is the official exam announcement. This announcement lists the training and experience qualifications. Check these standards and apply only if you come reasonably close to meeting them.

The brief description of the position in the examination announcement offers some clues to the subjects which will be tested. Think about the job itself. Review the duties in your mind. Can you perform them, or are there some in which you are rusty? Fill in the blank spots in your preparation.

Many jurisdictions preview the written test in the exam announcement by including a section called "Knowledge and Abilities Required," "Scope of the Examination," or some similar heading. Here you will find out specifically what fields will be tested.

2) Review your own background

Once you learn in general what the position is all about, and what you need to know to do the work, ask yourself which subjects you already know fairly well and which need improvement. You may wonder whether to concentrate on improving your strong areas or on building some background in your fields of weakness. When the announcement has specified "some knowledge" or "considerable knowledge," or has used adjectives like "beginning principles of…" or "advanced … methods," you can get a clue as to the number and difficulty of questions to be asked in any given field. More questions, and hence broader coverage, would be included for those subjects which are more important in the work. Now weigh your strengths and weaknesses against the job requirements and prepare accordingly.

3) Determine the level of the position

Another way to tell how intensively you should prepare is to understand the level of the job for which you are applying. Is it the entering level? In other words, is this the position in which beginners in a field of work are hired? Or is it an intermediate or advanced level? Sometimes this is indicated by such words as "Junior" or "Senior" in the class title. Other jurisdictions use Roman numerals to designate the level – Clerk I, Clerk II, for example. The word "Supervisor" sometimes appears in the title. If the level is not indicated by the title, check the description of duties. Will you be working under very close supervision, or will you have responsibility for independent decisions in this work?

4) Choose appropriate study materials

Now that you know the subjects to be examined and the relative amount of each subject to be covered, you can choose suitable study materials. For beginning level jobs, or even advanced ones, if you have a pronounced weakness in some aspect of your training, read a modern, standard textbook in that field. Be sure it is up to date and has general coverage. Such books are normally available at your library, and the librarian will be glad to help you locate one. For entry-level positions, questions of appropriate difficulty are chosen -- neither highly advanced questions, nor those too simple. Such questions require careful thought but not advanced training.

If the position for which you are applying is technical or advanced, you will read more advanced, specialized material. If you are already familiar with the basic principles of your field, elementary textbooks would waste your time. Concentrate on advanced textbooks and technical periodicals. Think through the concepts and review difficult problems in your field.

These are all general sources. You can get more ideas on your own initiative, following these leads. For example, training manuals and publications of the government agency which employs workers in your field can be useful, particularly for technical and professional positions. A letter or visit to the government department involved may result in more specific study suggestions, and certainly will provide you with a more definite idea of the exact nature of the position you are seeking.

III. KINDS OF TESTS

Tests are used for purposes other than measuring knowledge and ability to perform specified duties. For some positions, it is equally important to test ability to make adjustments to new situations or to profit from training. In others, basic mental abilities not dependent on information are essential. Questions which test these things may not appear as pertinent to the duties of the position as those which test for knowledge and information. Yet they are often highly important parts of a fair examination. For very general questions, it is almost impossible to help you direct your study efforts. What we can do is to point out some of the more common of these general abilities needed in public service positions and describe some typical questions.

1) General information

Broad, general information has been found useful for predicting job success in some kinds of work. This is tested in a variety of ways, from vocabulary lists to questions about current events. Basic background in some field of work, such as sociology or economics, may be sampled in a group of questions. Often these are principles which have become familiar to most persons through exposure rather than through formal training. It is difficult to advise you how to study for these questions; being alert to the world around you is our best suggestion.

2) Verbal ability

An example of an ability needed in many positions is verbal or language ability. Verbal ability is, in brief, the ability to use and understand words. Vocabulary and grammar tests are typical measures of this ability. Reading comprehension or paragraph interpretation questions are common in many kinds of civil service tests. You are given a paragraph of written material and asked to find its central meaning.

3) Numerical ability

Number skills can be tested by the familiar arithmetic problem, by checking paired lists of numbers to see which are alike and which are different, or by interpreting charts and graphs. In the latter test, a graph may be printed in the test booklet which you are asked to use as the basis for answering questions.

4) Observation

A popular test for law-enforcement positions is the observation test. A picture is shown to you for several minutes, then taken away. Questions about the picture test your ability to observe both details and larger elements.

5) Following directions

In many positions in the public service, the employee must be able to carry out written instructions dependably and accurately. You may be given a chart with several columns, each column listing a variety of information. The questions require you to carry out directions involving the information given in the chart.

6) Skills and aptitudes

Performance tests effectively measure some manual skills and aptitudes. When the skill is one in which you are trained, such as typing or shorthand, you can practice. These tests are often very much like those given in business school or high school courses. For many of the other skills and aptitudes, however, no short-time preparation can be made. Skills and abilities natural to you or that you have developed throughout your lifetime are being tested.

Many of the general questions just described provide all the data needed to answer the questions and ask you to use your reasoning ability to find the answers. Your best preparation for these tests, as well as for tests of facts and ideas, is to be at your physical and mental best. You, no doubt, have your own methods of getting into an exam-taking mood and keeping "in shape." The next section lists some ideas on this subject.

IV. KINDS OF QUESTIONS

Only rarely is the "essay" question, which you answer in narrative form, used in civil service tests. Civil service tests are usually of the short-answer type. Full instructions for answering these questions will be given to you at the examination. But in case this is your first experience with short-answer questions and separate answer sheets, here is what you need to know:

1) Multiple-choice Questions

Most popular of the short-answer questions is the "multiple choice" or "best answer" question. It can be used, for example, to test for factual knowledge, ability to solve problems or judgment in meeting situations found at work.

A multiple-choice question is normally one of three types—
- It can begin with an incomplete statement followed by several possible endings. You are to find the one ending which *best* completes the statement, although some of the others may not be entirely wrong.
- It can also be a complete statement in the form of a question which is answered by choosing one of the statements listed.

- It can be in the form of a problem – again you select the best answer.

Here is an example of a multiple-choice question with a discussion which should give you some clues as to the method for choosing the right answer:

When an employee has a complaint about his assignment, the action which will *best* help him overcome his difficulty is to
 A. discuss his difficulty with his coworkers
 B. take the problem to the head of the organization
 C. take the problem to the person who gave him the assignment
 D. say nothing to anyone about his complaint

In answering this question, you should study each of the choices to find which is best. Consider choice "A" – Certainly an employee may discuss his complaint with fellow employees, but no change or improvement can result, and the complaint remains unresolved. Choice "B" is a poor choice since the head of the organization probably does not know what assignment you have been given, and taking your problem to him is known as "going over the head" of the supervisor. The supervisor, or person who made the assignment, is the person who can clarify it or correct any injustice. Choice "C" is, therefore, correct. To say nothing, as in choice "D," is unwise. Supervisors have and interest in knowing the problems employees are facing, and the employee is seeking a solution to his problem.

2) True/False Questions

The "true/false" or "right/wrong" form of question is sometimes used. Here a complete statement is given. Your job is to decide whether the statement is right or wrong.

SAMPLE: A roaming cell-phone call to a nearby city costs less than a non-roaming call to a distant city.

This statement is wrong, or false, since roaming calls are more expensive.

This is not a complete list of all possible question forms, although most of the others are variations of these common types. You will always get complete directions for answering questions. Be sure you understand *how* to mark your answers – ask questions until you do.

V. RECORDING YOUR ANSWERS

Computer terminals are used more and more today for many different kinds of exams.

For an examination with very few applicants, you may be told to record your answers in the test booklet itself. Separate answer sheets are much more common. If this separate answer sheet is to be scored by machine – and this is often the case – it is highly important that you mark your answers correctly in order to get credit.

An electronic scoring machine is often used in civil service offices because of the speed with which papers can be scored. Machine-scored answer sheets must be marked with a pencil, which will be given to you. This pencil has a high graphite content which responds to the electronic scoring machine. As a matter of fact, stray dots may register as answers, so do not let your pencil rest on the answer sheet while you are pondering the correct answer. Also, if your pencil lead breaks or is otherwise defective, ask for another.

Since the answer sheet will be dropped in a slot in the scoring machine, be careful not to bend the corners or get the paper crumpled.

The answer sheet normally has five vertical columns of numbers, with 30 numbers to a column. These numbers correspond to the question numbers in your test booklet. After each number, going across the page are four or five pairs of dotted lines. These short dotted lines have small letters or numbers above them. The first two pairs may also have a "T" or "F" above the letters. This indicates that the first two pairs only are to be used if the questions are of the true-false type. If the questions are multiple choice, disregard the "T" and "F" and pay attention only to the small letters or numbers.

Answer your questions in the manner of the sample that follows:

32. The largest city in the United States is
    A. Washington, D.C.
    B. New York City
    C. Chicago
    D. Detroit
    E. San Francisco

1) Choose the answer you think is best. (New York City is the largest, so "B" is correct.)
2) Find the row of dotted lines numbered the same as the question you are answering. (Find row number 32)
3) Find the pair of dotted lines corresponding to the answer. (Find the pair of lines under the mark "B.")
4) Make a solid black mark between the dotted lines.

VI. BEFORE THE TEST

Common sense will help you find procedures to follow to get ready for an examination. Too many of us, however, overlook these sensible measures. Indeed, nervousness and fatigue have been found to be the most serious reasons why applicants fail to do their best on civil service tests. Here is a list of reminders:

- Begin your preparation early – Don't wait until the last minute to go scurrying around for books and materials or to find out what the position is all about.
- Prepare continuously – An hour a night for a week is better than an all-night cram session. This has been definitely established. What is more, a night a week for a month will return better dividends than crowding your study into a shorter period of time.
- Locate the place of the exam – You have been sent a notice telling you when and where to report for the examination. If the location is in a different town or otherwise unfamiliar to you, it would be well to inquire the best route and learn something about the building.
- Relax the night before the test – Allow your mind to rest. Do not study at all that night. Plan some mild recreation or diversion; then go to bed early and get a good night's sleep.
- Get up early enough to make a leisurely trip to the place for the test – This way unforeseen events, traffic snarls, unfamiliar buildings, etc. will not upset you.
- Dress comfortably – A written test is not a fashion show. You will be known by number and not by name, so wear something comfortable.

- Leave excess paraphernalia at home – Shopping bags and odd bundles will get in your way. You need bring only the items mentioned in the official notice you received; usually everything you need is provided. Do not bring reference books to the exam. They will only confuse those last minutes and be taken away from you when in the test room.
- Arrive somewhat ahead of time – If because of transportation schedules you must get there very early, bring a newspaper or magazine to take your mind off yourself while waiting.
- Locate the examination room – When you have found the proper room, you will be directed to the seat or part of the room where you will sit. Sometimes you are given a sheet of instructions to read while you are waiting. Do not fill out any forms until you are told to do so; just read them and be prepared.
- Relax and prepare to listen to the instructions
- If you have any physical problem that may keep you from doing your best, be sure to tell the test administrator. If you are sick or in poor health, you really cannot do your best on the exam. You can come back and take the test some other time.

VII. AT THE TEST

The day of the test is here and you have the test booklet in your hand. The temptation to get going is very strong. Caution! There is more to success than knowing the right answers. You must know how to identify your papers and understand variations in the type of short-answer question used in this particular examination. Follow these suggestions for maximum results from your efforts:

1) Cooperate with the monitor

The test administrator has a duty to create a situation in which you can be as much at ease as possible. He will give instructions, tell you when to begin, check to see that you are marking your answer sheet correctly, and so on. He is not there to guard you, although he will see that your competitors do not take unfair advantage. He wants to help you do your best.

2) Listen to all instructions

Don't jump the gun! Wait until you understand all directions. In most civil service tests you get more time than you need to answer the questions. So don't be in a hurry. Read each word of instructions until you clearly understand the meaning. Study the examples, listen to all announcements and follow directions. Ask questions if you do not understand what to do.

3) Identify your papers

Civil service exams are usually identified by number only. You will be assigned a number; you must not put your name on your test papers. Be sure to copy your number correctly. Since more than one exam may be given, copy your exact examination title.

4) Plan your time

Unless you are told that a test is a "speed" or "rate of work" test, speed itself is usually not important. Time enough to answer all the questions will be provided, but this does not mean that you have all day. An overall time limit has been set. Divide the total time (in minutes) by the number of questions to determine the approximate time you have for each question.

5) Do not linger over difficult questions

If you come across a difficult question, mark it with a paper clip (useful to have along) and come back to it when you have been through the booklet. One caution if you do this – be sure to skip a number on your answer sheet as well. Check often to be sure that you have not lost your place and that you are marking in the row numbered the same as the question you are answering.

6) Read the questions

Be sure you know what the question asks! Many capable people are unsuccessful because they failed to *read* the questions correctly.

7) Answer all questions

Unless you have been instructed that a penalty will be deducted for incorrect answers, it is better to guess than to omit a question.

8) Speed tests

It is often better NOT to guess on speed tests. It has been found that on timed tests people are tempted to spend the last few seconds before time is called in marking answers at random – without even reading them – in the hope of picking up a few extra points. To discourage this practice, the instructions may warn you that your score will be "corrected" for guessing. That is, a penalty will be applied. The incorrect answers will be deducted from the correct ones, or some other penalty formula will be used.

9) Review your answers

If you finish before time is called, go back to the questions you guessed or omitted to give them further thought. Review other answers if you have time.

10) Return your test materials

If you are ready to leave before others have finished or time is called, take ALL your materials to the monitor and leave quietly. Never take any test material with you. The monitor can discover whose papers are not complete, and taking a test booklet may be grounds for disqualification.

VIII. EXAMINATION TECHNIQUES

1) Read the general instructions carefully. These are usually printed on the first page of the exam booklet. As a rule, these instructions refer to the timing of the examination; the fact that you should not start work until the signal and must stop work at a signal, etc. If there are any *special* instructions, such as a choice of questions to be answered, make sure that you note this instruction carefully.

2) When you are ready to start work on the examination, that is as soon as the signal has been given, read the instructions to each question booklet, underline any key words or phrases, such as *least, best, outline, describe* and the like. In this way you will tend to answer as requested rather than discover on reviewing your paper that you *listed without describing*, that you selected the *worst* choice rather than the *best* choice, etc.

3) If the examination is of the objective or multiple-choice type – that is, each question will also give a series of possible answers: A, B, C or D, and you are called upon to select the best answer and write the letter next to that answer on your answer paper – it is advisable to start answering each question in turn. There may be anywhere from 50 to 100 such questions in the three or four hours allotted and you can see how much time would be taken if you read through all the questions before beginning to answer any. Furthermore, if you come across a question or group of questions which you know would be difficult to answer, it would undoubtedly affect your handling of all the other questions.

4) If the examination is of the essay type and contains but a few questions, it is a moot point as to whether you should read all the questions before starting to answer any one. Of course, if you are given a choice – say five out of seven and the like – then it is essential to read all the questions so you can eliminate the two that are most difficult. If, however, you are asked to answer all the questions, there may be danger in trying to answer the easiest one first because you may find that you will spend too much time on it. The best technique is to answer the first question, then proceed to the second, etc.

5) Time your answers. Before the exam begins, write down the time it started, then add the time allowed for the examination and write down the time it must be completed, then divide the time available somewhat as follows:
    - If 3-1/2 hours are allowed, that would be 210 minutes. If you have 80 objective-type questions, that would be an average of 2-1/2 minutes per question. Allow yourself no more than 2 minutes per question, or a total of 160 minutes, which will permit about 50 minutes to review.
    - If for the time allotment of 210 minutes there are 7 essay questions to answer, that would average about 30 minutes a question. Give yourself only 25 minutes per question so that you have about 35 minutes to review.

6) The most important instruction is to *read each question* and make sure you know what is wanted. The second most important instruction is to *time yourself properly* so that you answer every question. The third most important instruction is to *answer every question*. Guess if you have to but include something for each question. Remember that you will receive no credit for a blank and will probably receive some credit if you write something in answer to an essay question. If you guess a letter – say "B" for a multiple-choice question – you may have guessed right. If you leave a blank as an answer to a multiple-choice question, the examiners may respect your feelings but it will not add a point to your score. Some exams may penalize you for wrong answers, so in such cases *only*, you may not want to guess unless you have some basis for your answer.

7) Suggestions
    a. Objective-type questions
        1. Examine the question booklet for proper sequence of pages and questions
        2. Read all instructions carefully
        3. Skip any question which seems too difficult; return to it after all other questions have been answered
        4. Apportion your time properly; do not spend too much time on any single question or group of questions

5. Note and underline key words – *all, most, fewest, least, best, worst, same, opposite*, etc.
6. Pay particular attention to negatives
7. Note unusual option, e.g., unduly long, short, complex, different or similar in content to the body of the question
8. Observe the use of "hedging" words – *probably, may, most likely*, etc.
9. Make sure that your answer is put next to the same number as the question
10. Do not second-guess unless you have good reason to believe the second answer is definitely more correct
11. Cross out original answer if you decide another answer is more accurate; do not erase until you are ready to hand your paper in
12. Answer all questions; guess unless instructed otherwise
13. Leave time for review

b. Essay questions
1. Read each question carefully
2. Determine exactly what is wanted. Underline key words or phrases.
3. Decide on outline or paragraph answer
4. Include many different points and elements unless asked to develop any one or two points or elements
5. Show impartiality by giving pros and cons unless directed to select one side only
6. Make and write down any assumptions you find necessary to answer the questions
7. Watch your English, grammar, punctuation and choice of words
8. Time your answers; don't crowd material

8) Answering the essay question

Most essay questions can be answered by framing the specific response around several key words or ideas. Here are a few such key words or ideas:

M's: manpower, materials, methods, money, management
P's: purpose, program, policy, plan, procedure, practice, problems, pitfalls, personnel, public relations

a. Six basic steps in handling problems:
1. Preliminary plan and background development
2. Collect information, data and facts
3. Analyze and interpret information, data and facts
4. Analyze and develop solutions as well as make recommendations
5. Prepare report and sell recommendations
6. Install recommendations and follow up effectiveness

b. Pitfalls to avoid
1. *Taking things for granted* – A statement of the situation does not necessarily imply that each of the elements is necessarily true; for example, a complaint may be invalid and biased so that all that can be taken for granted is that a complaint has been registered

2. *Considering only one side of a situation* – Wherever possible, indicate several alternatives and then point out the reasons you selected the best one
3. *Failing to indicate follow up* – Whenever your answer indicates action on your part, make certain that you will take proper follow-up action to see how successful your recommendations, procedures or actions turn out to be
4. *Taking too long in answering any single question* – Remember to time your answers properly

IX. AFTER THE TEST

Scoring procedures differ in detail among civil service jurisdictions although the general principles are the same. Whether the papers are hand-scored or graded by machine we have described, they are nearly always graded by number. That is, the person who marks the paper knows only the number – never the name – of the applicant. Not until all the papers have been graded will they be matched with names. If other tests, such as training and experience or oral interview ratings have been given, scores will be combined. Different parts of the examination usually have different weights. For example, the written test might count 60 percent of the final grade, and a rating of training and experience 40 percent. In many jurisdictions, veterans will have a certain number of points added to their grades.

After the final grade has been determined, the names are placed in grade order and an eligible list is established. There are various methods for resolving ties between those who get the same final grade – probably the most common is to place first the name of the person whose application was received first. Job offers are made from the eligible list in the order the names appear on it. You will be notified of your grade and your rank as soon as all these computations have been made. This will be done as rapidly as possible.

People who are found to meet the requirements in the announcement are called "eligibles." Their names are put on a list of eligible candidates. An eligible's chances of getting a job depend on how high he stands on this list and how fast agencies are filling jobs from the list.

When a job is to be filled from a list of eligibles, the agency asks for the names of people on the list of eligibles for that job. When the civil service commission receives this request, it sends to the agency the names of the three people highest on this list. Or, if the job to be filled has specialized requirements, the office sends the agency the names of the top three persons who meet these requirements from the general list.

The appointing officer makes a choice from among the three people whose names were sent to him. If the selected person accepts the appointment, the names of the others are put back on the list to be considered for future openings.

That is the rule in hiring from all kinds of eligible lists, whether they are for typist, carpenter, chemist, or something else. For every vacancy, the appointing officer has his choice of any one of the top three eligibles on the list. This explains why the person whose name is on top of the list sometimes does not get an appointment when some of the persons lower on the list do. If the appointing officer chooses the second or third eligible, the No. 1 eligible does not get a job at once, but stays on the list until he is appointed or the list is terminated.

X. HOW TO PASS THE INTERVIEW TEST

The examination for which you applied requires an oral interview test. You have already taken the written test and you are now being called for the interview test – the final part of the formal examination.

You may think that it is not possible to prepare for an interview test and that there are no procedures to follow during an interview. Our purpose is to point out some things you can do in advance that will help you and some good rules to follow and pitfalls to avoid while you are being interviewed.

What is an interview supposed to test?

The written examination is designed to test the technical knowledge and competence of the candidate; the oral is designed to evaluate intangible qualities, not readily measured otherwise, and to establish a list showing the relative fitness of each candidate – as measured against his competitors – for the position sought. Scoring is not on the basis of "right" and "wrong," but on a sliding scale of values ranging from "not passable" to "outstanding." As a matter of fact, it is possible to achieve a relatively low score without a single "incorrect" answer because of evident weakness in the qualities being measured.

Occasionally, an examination may consist entirely of an oral test – either an individual or a group oral. In such cases, information is sought concerning the technical knowledges and abilities of the candidate, since there has been no written examination for this purpose. More commonly, however, an oral test is used to supplement a written examination.

Who conducts interviews?

The composition of oral boards varies among different jurisdictions. In nearly all, a representative of the personnel department serves as chairman. One of the members of the board may be a representative of the department in which the candidate would work. In some cases, "outside experts" are used, and, frequently, a businessman or some other representative of the general public is asked to serve. Labor and management or other special groups may be represented. The aim is to secure the services of experts in the appropriate field.

However the board is composed, it is a good idea (and not at all improper or unethical) to ascertain in advance of the interview who the members are and what groups they represent. When you are introduced to them, you will have some idea of their backgrounds and interests, and at least you will not stutter and stammer over their names.

What should be done before the interview?

While knowledge about the board members is useful and takes some of the surprise element out of the interview, there is other preparation which is more substantive. It *is* possible to prepare for an oral interview – in several ways:

1) Keep a copy of your application and review it carefully before the interview

This may be the only document before the oral board, and the starting point of the interview. Know what education and experience you have listed there, and the sequence and dates of all of it. Sometimes the board will ask you to review the highlights of your experience for them; you should not have to hem and haw doing it.

2) Study the class specification and the examination announcement

Usually, the oral board has one or both of these to guide them. The qualities, characteristics or knowledges required by the position sought are stated in these documents. They offer valuable clues as to the nature of the oral interview. For example, if the job involves supervisory responsibilities, the announcement will usually indicate that knowledge of modern supervisory methods and the qualifications of the candidate as a supervisor will be tested. If so, you can expect such questions, frequently in the form of a hypothetical situation which you are expected to solve. NEVER go into an oral without knowledge of the duties and responsibilities of the job you seek.

3) Think through each qualification required

Try to visualize the kind of questions you would ask if you were a board member. How well could you answer them? Try especially to appraise your own knowledge and background in each area, *measured against the job sought*, and identify any areas in which you are weak. Be critical and realistic – do not flatter yourself.

4) Do some general reading in areas in which you feel you may be weak

For example, if the job involves supervision and your past experience has NOT, some general reading in supervisory methods and practices, particularly in the field of human relations, might be useful. Do NOT study agency procedures or detailed manuals. The oral board will be testing your understanding and capacity, not your memory.

5) Get a good night's sleep and watch your general health and mental attitude

You will want a clear head at the interview. Take care of a cold or any other minor ailment, and of course, no hangovers.

What should be done on the day of the interview?

Now comes the day of the interview itself. Give yourself plenty of time to get there. Plan to arrive somewhat ahead of the scheduled time, particularly if your appointment is in the fore part of the day. If a previous candidate fails to appear, the board might be ready for you a bit early. By early afternoon an oral board is almost invariably behind schedule if there are many candidates, and you may have to wait. Take along a book or magazine to read, or your application to review, but leave any extraneous material in the waiting room when you go in for your interview. In any event, relax and compose yourself.

The matter of dress is important. The board is forming impressions about you – from your experience, your manners, your attitude, and your appearance. Give your personal appearance careful attention. Dress your best, but not your flashiest. Choose conservative, appropriate clothing, and be sure it is immaculate. This is a business interview, and your appearance should indicate that you regard it as such. Besides, being well groomed and properly dressed will help boost your confidence.

Sooner or later, someone will call your name and escort you into the interview room. *This is it.* From here on you are on your own. It is too late for any more preparation. But remember, you asked for this opportunity to prove your fitness, and you are here because your request was granted.

What happens when you go in?

The usual sequence of events will be as follows: The clerk (who is often the board stenographer) will introduce you to the chairman of the oral board, who will introduce you to the other members of the board. Acknowledge the introductions before you sit down. Do not be surprised if you find a microphone facing you or a stenotypist sitting by. Oral interviews are usually recorded in the event of an appeal or other review.

Usually the chairman of the board will open the interview by reviewing the highlights of your education and work experience from your application – primarily for the benefit of the other members of the board, as well as to get the material into the record. Do not interrupt or comment unless there is an error or significant misinterpretation; if that is the case, do not hesitate. But do not quibble about insignificant matters. Also, he will usually ask you some question about your education, experience or your present job – partly to get you to start talking and to establish the interviewing "rapport." He may start the actual questioning, or turn it over to one of the other members. Frequently, each member undertakes the questioning on a particular area, one in which he is perhaps most competent, so you can expect each member to participate in the examination. Because time is limited, you may also expect some rather abrupt switches in the direction the questioning takes, so do not be upset by it. Normally, a board member will not pursue a single line of questioning unless he discovers a particular strength or weakness.

After each member has participated, the chairman will usually ask whether any member has any further questions, then will ask you if you have anything you wish to add. Unless you are expecting this question, it may floor you. Worse, it may start you off on an extended, extemporaneous speech. The board is not usually seeking more information. The question is principally to offer you a last opportunity to present further qualifications or to indicate that you have nothing to add. So, if you feel that a significant qualification or characteristic has been overlooked, it is proper to point it out in a sentence or so. Do not compliment the board on the thoroughness of their examination – they have been sketchy, and you know it. If you wish, merely say, "No thank you, I have nothing further to add." This is a point where you can "talk yourself out" of a good impression or fail to present an important bit of information. Remember, *you close the interview yourself*.

The chairman will then say, "That is all, Mr. _____, thank you." Do not be startled; the interview is over, and quicker than you think. Thank him, gather your belongings and take your leave. Save your sigh of relief for the other side of the door.

How to put your best foot forward

Throughout this entire process, you may feel that the board individually and collectively is trying to pierce your defenses, seek out your hidden weaknesses and embarrass and confuse you. Actually, this is not true. They are obliged to make an appraisal of your qualifications for the job you are seeking, and they want to see you in your best light. Remember, they must interview all candidates and a non-cooperative candidate may become a failure in spite of their best efforts to bring out his qualifications. Here are 15 suggestions that will help you:

1) Be natural – Keep your attitude confident, not cocky

If you are not confident that you can do the job, do not expect the board to be. Do not apologize for your weaknesses, try to bring out your strong points. The board is interested in a positive, not negative, presentation. Cockiness will antagonize any board member and make him wonder if you are covering up a weakness by a false show of strength.

2) Get comfortable, but don't lounge or sprawl

Sit erectly but not stiffly. A careless posture may lead the board to conclude that you are careless in other things, or at least that you are not impressed by the importance of the occasion. Either conclusion is natural, even if incorrect. Do not fuss with your clothing, a pencil or an ashtray. Your hands may occasionally be useful to emphasize a point; do not let them become a point of distraction.

3) Do not wisecrack or make small talk

This is a serious situation, and your attitude should show that you consider it as such. Further, the time of the board is limited – they do not want to waste it, and neither should you.

4) Do not exaggerate your experience or abilities
In the first place, from information in the application or other interviews and sources, the board may know more about you than you think. Secondly, you probably will not get away with it. An experienced board is rather adept at spotting such a situation, so do not take the chance.

5) If you know a board member, do not make a point of it, yet do not hide it
Certainly you are not fooling him, and probably not the other members of the board. Do not try to take advantage of your acquaintanceship – it will probably do you little good.

6) Do not dominate the interview
Let the board do that. They will give you the clues – do not assume that you have to do all the talking. Realize that the board has a number of questions to ask you, and do not try to take up all the interview time by showing off your extensive knowledge of the answer to the first one.

7) Be attentive
You only have 20 minutes or so, and you should keep your attention at its sharpest throughout. When a member is addressing a problem or question to you, give him your undivided attention. Address your reply principally to him, but do not exclude the other board members.

8) Do not interrupt
A board member may be stating a problem for you to analyze. He will ask you a question when the time comes. Let him state the problem, and wait for the question.

9) Make sure you understand the question
Do not try to answer until you are sure what the question is. If it is not clear, restate it in your own words or ask the board member to clarify it for you. However, do not haggle about minor elements.

10) Reply promptly but not hastily
A common entry on oral board rating sheets is "candidate responded readily," or "candidate hesitated in replies." Respond as promptly and quickly as you can, but do not jump to a hasty, ill-considered answer.

11) Do not be peremptory in your answers
A brief answer is proper – but do not fire your answer back. That is a losing game from your point of view. The board member can probably ask questions much faster than you can answer them.

12) Do not try to create the answer you think the board member wants
He is interested in what kind of mind you have and how it works – not in playing games. Furthermore, he can usually spot this practice and will actually grade you down on it.

13) Do not switch sides in your reply merely to agree with a board member
Frequently, a member will take a contrary position merely to draw you out and to see if you are willing and able to defend your point of view. Do not start a debate, yet do not surrender a good position. If a position is worth taking, it is worth defending.

14) Do not be afraid to admit an error in judgment if you are shown to be wrong
The board knows that you are forced to reply without any opportunity for careful consideration. Your answer may be demonstrably wrong. If so, admit it and get on with the interview.

15) Do not dwell at length on your present job
The opening question may relate to your present assignment. Answer the question but do not go into an extended discussion. You are being examined for a *new* job, not your present one. As a matter of fact, try to phrase ALL your answers in terms of the job for which you are being examined.

Basis of Rating
Probably you will forget most of these "do's" and "don'ts" when you walk into the oral interview room. Even remembering them all will not ensure you a passing grade. Perhaps you did not have the qualifications in the first place. But remembering them will help you to put your best foot forward, without treading on the toes of the board members.

Rumor and popular opinion to the contrary notwithstanding, an oral board wants you to make the best appearance possible. They know you are under pressure – but they also want to see how you respond to it as a guide to what your reaction would be under the pressures of the job you seek. They will be influenced by the degree of poise you display, the personal traits you show and the manner in which you respond.

ABOUT THIS BOOK

This book contains tests divided into Examination Sections. Go through each test, answering every question in the margin. We have also attached a sample answer sheet at the back of the book that can be removed and used. At the end of each test look at the answer key and check your answers. On the ones you got wrong, look at the right answer choice and learn. Do not fill in the answers first. Do not memorize the questions and answers, but understand the answer and principles involved. On your test, the questions will likely be different from the samples. Questions are changed and new ones added. If you understand these past questions you should have success with any changes that arise. Tests may consist of several types of questions. We have additional books on each subject should more study be advisable or necessary for you. Finally, the more you study, the better prepared you will be. This book is intended to be the last thing you study before you walk into the examination room. Prior study of relevant texts is also recommended. NLC publishes some of these in our Fundamental Series. Knowledge and good sense are important factors in passing your exam. Good luck also helps. So now study this Passbook, absorb the material contained within and take that knowledge into the examination. Then do your best to pass that exam.

EXAMINATION SECTION

EXAMINATION SECTION
TEST 1

DIRECTIONS: Each question or incomplete statement is followed by several suggested answers or completions. Select the one that BEST answers the question or completes the statement. *PRINT THE LETTER OF THE CORRECT ANSWER IN THE SPACE AT THE RIGHT.*

1. Assume that a few co-workers meet near your desk and talk about personal matters during working hours. Lately, this practice has interfered with your work.
   In order to stop this practice, the BEST action for you to take FIRST is to
   A. ask your supervisor to put a stop to the co-workers' meeting near your desk
   B. discontinue any friendship with this group
   C. ask your co-workers not to meet near your desk
   D. request that your desk be moved to another location

   1.____

2. In order to maintain office coverage during working hours, your supervisor has scheduled your lunch hour from 1 P.M. to 2 P.M. and your co-workers' lunch hour from 12 P.M. to 1 P.M. Lately, your co-worker has been returning late from lunch each day. As a result, you don't get a full hour since you must return to the office by 2 P.M.
   Of the following, the BEST action for you to take FIRST is to
   A. explain to your co-worker in a courteous manner that his lateness is interfering with your right to a full hour for lunch
   B. tell your co-worker that his lateness must stop or you will report him to your supervisor
   C. report your co-worker's lateness to your supervisor
   D. leave at 1 P.M. for lunch, whether your co-worker has returned or not

   2.____

3. Assume that, as an office worker, one of your jobs is to open mail sent to your unit, read the mail for content, and send the mail to the appropriate person to handle. You accidentally open and begin to read a letter marked *personal* to a co-worker.
   Of the following, the BEST action for you to take is to
   A. report to your supervisor that your co-worker is receiving personal mail at the office
   B. destroy the letter so that your co-worker does not know you saw it
   C. reseal the letter and place it on the co-worker's desk without saying anything
   D. bring the letter to your co-worker and explain that you opened it by accident

   3.____

4. Suppose that in evaluating your work, your supervisor gives you an overall rating, but states that you sometimes turn in work with careless errors.
   The BEST action for you to take would be to
   A. ask a co-worker who is good at details to proofread your work
   B. take time to do a careful job, paying more attention to detail
   C. continue working as usual since occasional errors are to be expected
   D. ask your supervisor if she would mind correcting your errors

4.____

5. Assume that you are taking a telephone message for a co-worker who is not in the office at the time.
   Of the following, the LEAST important item to write on the message is the
   A. length of the call   B. name of the caller
   C. time of the call   D. telephone number of the caller

5.____

Questions 6-13.

DIRECTIONS: Questions 6 through 13 each consist of a sentence which may or may not be an example of good English. The underlined parts of each sentence may be correct or incorrect. Examine each sentence, considering grammar, punctuation, spelling, and capitalization. If the English usage in the underlined parts of the sentence given is better than any of the changes in the underlined words suggested in Options B, C, or D, choose Option A. If the changes in the underlined words suggested in Options B, C, or D would make the sentence correct, choose the correct option. Do not choose an option that will change the meaning of the sentence.

6. This Fall, the office will be closed on Columbus Day, October 9th
   A. Correct as is   B. fall...Columbus Day, October
   C. Fall...Columbus day, October   D. fall...Columbus Day, october

6.____

7. This manual discribes the duties performed by an Office Aide.
   A. Correct as is   B. describe the duties performed
   C. discribe the duties performed   D. describes the duties performed

7.____

8. There weren't no paper in the supply closet.
   A. Correct as is   B. weren't any
   C. wasn't any   D. wasn't no

8.____

9. The new employees left there office to attend a meeting.
   A. Correct as is   B. they're
   C. their   D. thier

9.____

10. The office worker started working at 8:30 a.m.
    A. Correct as is   B. 8:30 a.m.
    C. 8;30 a,m.   D. 8:30 am.

10.____

11. The alphabet, or A to Z sequence are the basis of most filing systems.
    A. Correct as is   B. alphabet, or A to Z sequence, is
    C. alphabet, or A to Z sequence are   D. alphabet, or A too Z sequence, is

11.____

12. <u>Those</u> file cabinets are five <u>feet</u> tall. 12.____
    A. Correct as is   B. Them…feet
    C. Those…foot   D. Them…foot

13. The Office Aide checked the <u>register and finding</u> the date of the meeting. 13.____
    A. Correct as is   B. regaster and finding
    C. register and found   D. regaster and found

Questions 14-21.

DIRECTIONS: Each of Questions 14 through 21 has two lists of numbers. Each list contains three sets of numbers. Check each of the three sets in the list on the right to see if they are the same as the corresponding set in the list on the left. Mark your answers
   A. if none of the sets in the right list are the same as those in the left list
   B. if only one of the sets in the right list are the same as those in the left list
   C. if only two of the sets in the right list are the same as those in the left list
   D. if all three sets in the right list are the same as those in the left list

14. 7354183476   7354983476   14.____
    4474747744   4474747774
    57914302311   57914302311

15. 7143592185   7143892185   15.____
    8344517699   8344518699
    9178531263   9178531263

16. 2572114731   257214731   16.____
    8806835476   8806835476
    8255831246   8255831246

17. 331476853821   331476858621   17.____
    6976658532996   6976655832996
    3766042113715   3766042113745

18. 8806663315   8806663315   18.____
    74477138449   74477138449
    211756663666   211756663666

19. 990006966996   99000696996   19.____
    53022219743   53022219843
    4171171117717   4171171177717

20. 24400222433004 24400222433004   20.____
    5300030055000355 5300030055500355
    20000075532002022 20000075532002022

21. 6111666406600011116   61116664066001116   21._____
     7111300117001100733   7111300117001100733
     26666446664476518   26666446664476518

Questions 22-25.

DIRECTIONS: Each of Questions 22 through 25 has two lists of names and addresses. Each
             list contains three sets of names and addresses. Check each of the three sets
             in the list on the right to see if they are the same as the corresponding set in
             the list on the left. Mark your answers
                A. if none of the sets in the right list are the same as those in the left list
                B. if only one of the sets in the right list are the same as those in the left list
                C. if only two of the sets in the right list are the same as those in the left list
                D. if all three sets in the right list are the same as those in the left list

22. Mary T. Berlinger   Mary T. Berlinger   22._____
     2351 Hampton St.   2351 Hampton St.
     Monsey, N.Y. 20117   Monsey, N.Y. 20117

     Eduardo Benes   Eduardo Benes
     473 Kingston Avenue   473 Kingston Avenue
     Central Islip, N.Y. 11734   Central Islip, N.Y. 11734

     Alan Carrington Fuchs   Alan Carrington Fuchs
     17 Gnarled Hollow Road   17 Gnarled Hollow Road
     Los Angeles, CA 91635   Los Angeles, CA 91685

23. David John Jacobson   David John Jacobson   23._____
     178 35 St. Apt. 4C   178 53 St. Apt. 4C
     New York, N.Y. 00927   New York, N.Y. 00927

     Ann-Marie Calonella   Ann-Marie Calonella
     7243 South Ridge Blvd.   7243 South Ridge Blvd.
     Bakersfield, CA 96714   Bakersfield, CA 96714

     Pauline M. Thompson   Pauline M. Thomson
     872 Linden Ave.   872 Linden Ave.
     Houston, Texas 70321   Houston, Texas 70321

24. Chester LeRoy Masterton   Chester LeRoy Masterson   24._____
     152 Lacy Rd.   152 Lacy Rd.
     Kankakee, Ill. 54532   Kankakee, Ill. 54532

     William Maloney   William Maloney
     S. LaCrosse Pla.   S. LaCross Pla.
     Wausau, Wisconsin 52146   Wausau, Wisconsin 52146

Cynthia V. Barnes
16 Pines Rd.
Greenpoint, Miss. 20376

Cynthia V. Barnes
16 Pines Rd.
Greenpoint, Miss. 20376

25. Marcel Jean Frontenac
6 Burton On The Water
Calender, Me. 01471

Marcel Jean Frontenac
6 Burton On The Water
Calender, Me. 01471

25._____

J. Scott Marsden
174 S. Tipton St.
Cleveland, Ohio

J. Scott Marsden
174 Tipton St.
Cleveland, Ohio

Lawrence T. Haney
171 McDonough St.
Decatur, Ga. 31304

Lawrence T. Haney
171 McDonough St.
Decatur, Ga. 31304

KEY (CORRECT ANSWERS)

1.	C		11.	B
2.	A		12.	A
3.	D		13.	C
4.	B		14.	B
5.	A		15.	B
6.	B		16.	C
7.	D		17.	A
8.	C		18.	D
9.	C		19.	A
10.	B		20.	C

21. C
22. C
23. B
24. B
25. C

TEST 2

DIRECTIONS: Each question or incomplete statement is followed by several suggested answers or completions. Select the one that BEST answers the question or completes the statement. *PRINT THE LETTER OF THE CORRECT ANSWER IN THE SPACE AT THE RIGHT.*

Questions 1-6.

DIRECTIONS: Questions 1 through 6 are to be answered SOLELY on the basis of the information contained in the following passage.

Duplicating is the process of making a number of identical copies of letters, document, etc. from an original. Some duplicating processes make copies directly from the original document. Other duplicating processes require the preparation of a special master, and copies are then made from the master. Four of the most common duplicating processes are stencil, fluid, offset, and xerox.

In the stencil process, the typewriter is used to cut the words into a master called a stencil. Drawings, charts, or graphs can be cut into the stencil using a stylus. As many as 3,500 good-quality copies can be reproduced from one stencil. Various grades of finished paper from inexpensive mimeograph to expensive bond can be used.

The fluid process is a good method of copying from 50 to 125 good-quality copies from a master, which is prepared with a special dye. The master is placed on the duplicator, and special paper with a hard finish is moistened and then passed through the duplicator. Some of the dye on the master is dissolved, creating an impression on the paper. The impression becomes lighter as more copies are made; and once the dye on the master is used up, a new master must be made.

The offset process is the most adaptable office duplicating process because this process can be used for making a few copies or many copies. Masters can be made on paper or plastic for a few hundred copies, or on metal plates for as many as 75,000 copies. By using a special technique called photo-offset, charts, photographs, illustrations, or graphs can be reproduced on the master plate. The offset process is capable of producing large quantities of fine, top-quality copies on all types of finished paper.

The xerox process reproduces an exact duplicate from an original. It is the fastest duplicating method because the original material is placed directly on the duplicator, eliminating the need to make a special master. Any kind of paper can be used. The xerox process is the most expensive duplicating process; however, it is the best method of reproducing small quantities of good-quality copies of reports, letters, official documents, memos, or contracts.

1. Of the following, the MOST efficient method of reproducing 5,000 copies of a graph is 1._____
    A. stencil   B. fluid   C. offset   D. xerox

2. The offset process is the MOST adaptable office duplicating process because
    A. it is the quickest duplicating method
    B. it is the least expensive duplicating method
    C. it can produce a small number or large number of copies
    D. a softer master can be used over and over again

3. Which one of the following duplicating processes uses moistened paper?
    A. Stencil B. Fluid C. Offset D. Xerox

4. The fluid process would be the BEST process to use for reproducing
    A. five copies of a school transcript
    B. fifty copies of a memo
    C. five hundred copies of a form letter
    D. five thousand copies of a chart

5. Which one of the following duplicating processes does NOT require a special master?
    A. Fluid B. Xerox C. Offset D. Stencil

6. Xerox is NOT used for all duplicating jobs because
    A. it produces poor-quality copies
    B. the process is too expensive
    C. preparing the master is too time-consuming
    D. it cannot produce written reports

7. Assume a city agency has 775 office workers.
    If 2 out of 25 office workers were absent on a particular day, how many office workers reported to work on that day?
    A. 713 B. 744 C. 750 D. 773

Questions 8-11.

DIRECTIONS: In Questions 8 through 11, select the choice that is CLOSEST in meaning to the underlined word.

SAMPLE: This division reviews the fiscal reports of the agency.
In this sentence, the word *fiscal* means MOST NEARLY
A. financial B. critical C. basic D. personnel

The correct answer is A, financial, because financial is closest to *fiscal*.

8. A central file eliminates the need to retain duplicate material.
    The word *retain* means MOST NEARLY
    A. keep B. change C. locate D. process

9. Filing is a routine office task.
    Routine means MOST NEARLY
    A. proper B. regular C. simple D. difficult

10. Sometimes a word, phrase, or sentence must be <u>deleted</u> to correct an error. 10.____
    Deleted means MOST NEARLY
    A. removed   B. added   C. expanded   D. improved

11. Your supervisor will <u>evaluate</u> your work. 11.____
    Evaluate means MOST NEARLY
    A. judge   B. list   C. assign   D. explain

Questions 12-19.

DIRECTIONS: The code table below shows 10 letters with matching numbers. For each Question 12 through 19, there are three sets of letters. Each set of letters is followed by a set of numbers which may or may not match their correct letter according to the code table. For each question, check all three sets of letters and numbers and mark your answer
   A. if no pairs are correctly matched
   B. if only one pair is correctly matched
   C. if only two pairs are correctly matched
   D. if all three pairs are correctly matched

CODE TABLE

T	M	V	D	S	P	R	G	B	H
1	2	3	4	5	6	7	8	9	0

SAMPLE QUESTION: TMVDSP   123456
                   RGBHTM   789011
                   DSPRGB   256780

In the sample question above, the first set of numbers correctly matches its set of letters. But the second and third pairs contain mistakes. In the second pair, M is incorrectly matched with number 1. According to the code table, letter M should be correctly matched with number 2. In the third pair, the letter D is incorrectly matched with number 2. According to the code table, letter D should be correctly matched with number 4. Since only one of the pairs is correctly matched, the answer to this sample question is B.

12. RSBMRM   759262   12.____
     GDSRVH   845730
     VDBRTM   349713

13. TGVSDR   183247   13.____
     SMHRDP   520647
     TRMHSR   172057

14. DSPRGM   456782   14.____
     MVDBHT   234902
     HPMDBT   062491

15. BVPTRD   936184   15._____
     GDPHMB   807029
     GMRHMV   827032

16. MGVRSH   283750   16._____
     TRDMBS   174295
     SPRMGV   567283

17. SGBSDM   489542   17._____
     MGHPTM   290612
     MPBMHT   269301

18. TDPBHM   146902   18._____
     VPBMRS   369275
     GDMBHM   842902

19. MVPTBV   236194   19._____
     PDRTMB   647128
     BGTMSM   981232

Questions 20-25.

DIRECTIONS: In each of Questions 20 through 25, the names of four people are given. For each question, choose as your answer the one of the four names given which should be filed FIRST according to the usual system of alphabetical filing of names, as described in the following paragraph.

In filing names, you must start with the last name. Names are filed in order of the first letter of the last name, then the second letter, etc. Therefore, BAILY would be filed before BROWN, which would be filed before COLT. A name with fewer letters of the same type comes first; i.e., Smith before Smithe. If the last names are the same, the names are filed alphabetically by the first name. If the first name is an initial, a name with an initial would come before a first name that starts with the same letter as the initial. Therefore, I. BROWN would come before IRA BROWN. Finally, if both last name and first name are the same, the name would be filed alphabetically by the middle name, one again an initial coming before a middle name which starts with the same letter as the initial. If there is no middle name at all, the name would come before those with middle initials or names.

SAMPLE QUESTION: A. Lester Daniels
                   B. William Dancer
                   C. Nathan Danzig
                   D. Dan Lester

The last names beginning with D are filed before the last name beginning with L. Since DANIELS, DANCER, and DANZIG all begin with the same three letters, you must look at the fourth letter of the last name to determine which name should be filed first. C comes before I or Z in the alphabet, so DANCER is filed before DANIELS or DANZIG. Therefore, the answer to the above sample question is B.

20. A. Scott Biala   B. Mary Byala   20.____
     C. Martin Baylor   D. Francis Bauer

21. A. Howard J. Black   B. Howard Black   21.____
     C. J. Howard Black   D. John H. Black

22. A. Theodora Garth Kingston   B. Theadore Barth Kingston   22.____
     C. Thomas Kingston   D. Thomas T. Kingston

23. A. Paulette Mary Huerta B. Paul M. Huerta   23.____
     C. Paulette L. Huerta   D. Peter A. Huerta

24. A. Martha Hunt Morgan   B. Martin Hunt Morgan   24.____
     C. Mary H. Morgan   D. Martine H. Morgan

25. A. James T. Meerschaum B. James M. Mershum   25.____
     C. James F. Mearshaum   D. James N. Meshum

KEY (CORRECT ANSWERS)

1.	C	11.	A
2.	C	12.	B
3.	B	13.	B
4.	B	14.	C
5.	B	15.	A
6.	B	16.	D
7.	A	17.	A
8.	A	18.	D
9.	B	19.	A
10.	A	20.	D

21. B
22. B
23. B
24. A
25. C

TEST 3

DIRECTIONS: Each question or incomplete statement is followed by several suggested answers or completions. Select the one that BEST answers the question or completes the statement. *PRINT THE LETTER OF THE CORRECT ANSWER IN THE SPACE AT THE RIGHT.*

1. Which one of the following statements about proper telephone usage is NOT always correct?
   When answering the telephone, you should
   A. know whom you are speaking to
   B. give the caller your undivided attention
   C. identify yourself to the caller
   D. obtain the information the caller wishes before you do your other work

   1.____

2. Assume that, as a member of a worker's safety committee in your agency, you are responsible for encouraging other employees to follow correct safety practices. While you are working on your regular assignment, you observe an employee violating a safety rule.
   Of the following, the BEST action for you to take FIRST is to
   A. speak to the employee about safety practices and order him to stop violating the safety rule
   B. speak to the employee about safety practices and point out the safety rule he is violating
   C. bring the matter up in the next committee meeting
   D. report this violation of the safety rule to the employee's supervisor

   2.____

3. Assume that you have been temporarily assigned by your supervisor to do a job which you do not want to do.
   The BEST action for you to take is to
   A. discuss the job with your supervisor, explaining why you do not want to do it
   B. discuss the job with your supervisor and tell her that you will not do it
   C. ask a co-worker to take your place on this job
   D. do some other job that you like; your supervisor may give the job you do not like to someone else

   3.____

4. Assume that you keep the confidential personnel files of employees in your unit. A friend asks you to obtain some information from the file of one of your co-workers.
   The BEST action to take is to _____ to your friend.
   A. ask the co-worker if you can give the information
   B. ask your supervisor if you can give the information
   C. give the information
   D. refuse to give the information

   4.____

Questions 5-8.

DIRECTIONS: Questions 5 through 8 are to be answered SOLELY on the basis of the information contained in the following passage.

City government is committed to providing a safe and healthy work environment for all city employees. An effective agency safety program reduces accidents by educating employees about the types of careless acts which can cause accidents. Even in an office, accidents can happen. If each employee is aware of possible safety hazards, the number of accidents on the job can be reduced.

Careless use of office equipment can cause accidents and injuries. For example, file cabinet drawers which are filled with papers can be so heavy that the entire cabinet could tip over from the weight of one open drawer.

The bottom drawers of desks and file cabinets should never be left open since employees can easily trip over open drawers and injure themselves.

When reaching for objects on a high shelf, an employee should use a strong, sturdy object such as a stepstool to stand on. Makeshift platforms made out of books, papers, or boxes can easily collapse. Even chairs can slide out from under foot, causing serious injury.

Even at an employee's desk, safety hazards can occur. Frayed or cut wires should be repaired or replaced immediately. Computers which are not firmly anchored to the desk or table could fall, causing injury.

Smoking is one of the major causes of fires in the office. A lighted match or improperly extinguished cigarette thrown into a wastebasket filled with paper could cause a major fire with possible loss of life. Where smoking is permitted, ashtrays should be used. Smoking is particularly dangerous in offices were flammable chemicals are used.

5. The goal of an effective safety program is to
   A. reduce office accidents
   B. stop employees from smoking on the job
   C. encourage employees to continue their education
   D. eliminate high shelves in offices

6. Desks and file cabinets can become safety hazards when
   A. their drawers are left open
   B. they are used as wastebaskets
   C. they are makeshift
   D. they are not anchored securely to the floor

7. Smoking is especially hazardous when it occurs
   A. near exposed wires
   B. in a crowded office
   C. in an area where flammable chemicals are used
   D. where books and papers are stored

8. Accidents are likely to occur when
   A. employees' desks are cluttered with books and papers
   B. employees are not aware of safety hazards
   C. employees close desk drawers
   D. stepstools are used to reach high objects

9. Assume that part of your job as a worker in the accounting division of a city agency is to answer the telephone.
When you first answer the telephone, it is LEAST important to tell the caller
   A. your title
   B. your name
   C. the name of your unit
   D. the name of your agency

9._____

10. Assume that you are assigned to work as a receptionist, and your duties are to answer phones, greet visitors, and do other general office work. You are busy with a routine job when several visitors approach your desk.
The BEST action to take is to
   A. ask the visitors to have a seat and assist them after your work is completed
   B. tell the visitors that you are busy and they should return at a more convenient time
   C. stop working long enough to assist the visitors
   D. continue working and wait for the visitors to ask you for assistance

10._____

11. Assume that your supervisor has chosen you to take a special course during hours to learn a new payroll procedure. Although you know that you were chosen because of your good work record, a co-worker, who feels that he should have been chosen, has been telling everyone in your unit that the choice was unfair.
Of the following, the BEST way to handle this situation FIRST is to
   A. suggest to the co-worker that everything in life is unfair
   B. contact your union representative in case your co-worker presents a formal grievance
   C. tell your supervisor about your co-worker's complaints and let her handle the situation
   D. tell the co-worker that you were chosen because of your superior work record

11._____

12. Assume that while you are working on an assignment which must be completed quickly, a supervisor from another unit asks you to obtain information for her.
Of the following, the BEST way to respond to her request is to
   A. tell her to return in an hour since you are busy
   B. give her the names of some people in her own unit who could help her
   C. tell her you are busy and refer her to a co-worker
   D. tell her that you are busy and ask her if she could wait until you finish your assignment

12._____

13. A co-worker in your unit is often off from work because of illness. Your supervisor assigns the co-worker's work to you when she is not there. Lately, doing her work has interfered with your own job.
The BEST action for you to take FIRST is to
   A. discuss the problem with your supervisor
   B. complete your own work before starting your co-worker's work
   C. ask other workers in your unit to assist you
   D. work late in order to get the jobs done

13._____

14. During the month of June, 40,587 people attended a city-owned swimming pool. In July, 13,014 more people attended the swimming pool than the number that had attended in June. In August, 39,655 people attended the swimming pool. The TOTAL number of people who attended the swimming pool during the months of June, July, and August was 14._____
   A. 80,242   B. 93,256   C. 133,843   D. 210,382

Questions 15-22.

DIRECTIONS: Questions 15 through 22 test how well you understand what you read. It will be necessary for you to read carefully because your answers to these questions must be based ONLY on the information in the following paragraphs.

   The telephone directory is made up of two books. The first book consists of the introductory section and the alphabetical listing of names section. The second book is the classified directory (also known as the yellow pages). Many people who are familiar with one book do not realize how useful the other can be. The efficient office worker should become familiar with both books in order to make the best use of this important source of information.
   The introductory section gives general instructions for finding numbers in the alphabetical listing and classified directory. This section also explains how to use the telephone company's many services, including the operator and information services, gives examples of charges for local and long-distance calls, and lists area codes for the entire country. In addition, this section provides a useful zip code map.
   The alphabetical listing of names section lists the names, addresses, and telephone numbers of subscribers in an area. Guide names, or *telltales*, are on the top corner of each page. These guide names indicate the first and last name to be found on that page. *Telltales* help locate any particular name quickly. A cross-reference spelling is also given to help locate names which are spelled several different ways. City, state, and federal government agencies are listed under the major government heading. For example, an agency of the federal government would be listed under *United States Government*.
   The classified directory, or yellow pages, is a separate book. In this section are advertising services, public transportation line maps, shopping guides, and listings of businesses arranged by the type of product or services they offer. This book is most useful when looking for the name or phone number of a business when all that is known is the type of product offered and the address, or when trying to locate a particular type of business in an area. Businesses listed in the classified directory can usually be found in the alphabetical listing of names section. When the name of the business is known, you will find the address or phone number more quickly in the alphabetical listing of names section.

15. The introductory section provides 15._____
   A. shopping guides   B. government listings
   C. business listings   D. information services

16. Advertising services would be found in the 16._____
   A. introductory section   B. alphabetical listing of names section\
   C. classified directory   D. information services

17. According to the information in the above passage for locating government agencies, the Information Office of the Department of Consumer Affairs of New York City government would be alphabetically listed FIRST under
    A. *I* for Information Offices
    B. *D* for Department of Consumer Affairs
    C. *N* for New York City
    D. *G* for government

17.____

18. When the name of a business is known, the QUICKEST way to find the phone number is to look in the
    A. classified directory
    B. introductory section
    C. alphabetical listing of name section
    D. advertising service section

18.____

19. The QUICKEST way to find the phone number of a business when the type of service a business offers and its address is known is to look in the
    A. classified directory
    B. alphabetical listing of names section
    C. introductory section
    D. information service

19.____

20. What is a *telltale*?
    A. An alphabetical listing   B. A guide name
    C. A map   D. A cross-reference listing

20.____

21. The BEST way to find a postal zip code is to look in the
    A. classified directory
    B. introductory section
    C. alphabetical listing of names section
    D. government heading

21.____

22. To help find names which have several different spellings, the telephone directory provides
    A. cross-reference spelling   B. *telltales*
    C. spelling guides   D. advertising services

22.____

23. Assume that your agency has been given $2,025 to purchase file cabinets. If each file cabinet costs $135, how many file cabinet can your agency purchase?
    A. 8   B. 10   C. 15   D. 16

23.____

24. Assume that your unit ordered 14 staplers at a total cost of $30.20 and each stapler cost the same.
    The cost of one stapler was MOST NEARLY
    A. $1.02   B. $1.61   C. $2.16   D. $2.26

24.____

25. Assume that you are responsible for counting and recording licensing fees collected by your department. On a particular day, your department collected in fees 40 checks in the amount of $6 each, 80 checks in the amount of $4 each, 45 twenty dollar bills, 30 ten dollar bills, 42 five dollar bills, and 186 one dollar bills.
The TOTAL amount in fees collected on that day was
   A. $1,406   B. $1,706   C. $2,156   D. $2,356

26. Assume that you are responsible for your agency's petty cash fund. During the month of February, you pay out 7 $2.00 subway fares and one taxi fare for $10.85. You pay out nothing else from the fund. At the end of February, you count the money left in the fund and find 3 one dollar bills, 4 quarters, 5 dimes, and 4 nickels.
The amount of money you had available in the petty cash fund at the BEGINNING of February was
   A. $4.70   B. $16.35   C. $24.85   D. $29.55

27. You overhear your supervisor criticize a co-worker for handling equipment in an unsafe way. You feel that the criticism may be unfair.
Of the following, it would be BEST for you to
   A. take your co-worker aside and tell her how you feel about your supervisor's comments
   B. interrupt the discussion and defend your co-worker to your supervisor
   C. continue working as if you had not overheard the discussion
   D. make a list of other workers who have violated safety rules and give it to your supervisor

28. Assume that you have been assigned to work on a long-term project with an employee who is known for being uncooperative.
In beginning to work with this employee, it would be LEAST desirable for you to
   A. understand why the person is uncooperative
   B. act in a calm manner rather than an emotional manner
   C. be appreciative of the co-worker's work
   D. report the co-worker's lack of cooperation to your supervisor

29. Assume that you are assigned to sell tickets at a city-owned ice skating rink. An adult ticket costs $4.50, and a children's ticket costs $2.25. At the end of a day, you find that you have sold 36 adult tickets and 80 children's tickets.
The TOTAL amount of money you collected for that day was
   A. $244.80   B. $318.00   C. $342.00   D. $348.00

30. If each office worker files 487 index cards in one hour, how many card can 26 office workers file in one hour?
   A. 10,662   B. 12,175   C. 12,662   D. 14,266

KEY (CORRECT ANSWERS)

1.	D	11.	C	21.	B
2.	B	12.	D	22.	A
3.	A	13.	A	23.	C
4.	D	14.	C	24.	C
5.	A	15.	D	25.	C
6.	A	16.	C	26.	D
7.	C	17.	C	27.	C
8.	B	18.	C	28.	D
9.	A	19.	A	29.	C
10.	C	20.	B	30.	C

EXAMINATION SECTION
TEST 1

DIRECTIONS: Each question or incomplete statement is followed by several suggested answers or completions. Select the one that BEST answers the question or completes the statement. *PRINT THE LETTER OF THE CORRECT ANSWER IN THE SPACE AT THE RIGHT.*

1. If you open a personal letter by mistake, the one of the following actions which it would generally be BEST for you to take is to

    A. ignore your error, attach the envelope to the letter, and distribute in the usual manner
    B. personally give the addressee the letter without any explanation
    C. place the letter inside the envelope, indicate under your initials that it was opened in error, and give to the addressee
    D. reseal the envelope or place the contents in another envelope and pass on to addressee

    1._____

2. If you receive a telephone call regarding a matter which your office does not handle, you should FIRST

    A. give the caller the telephone number of the proper office so that he can dial again
    B. offer to transfer the caller to the proper office
    C. suggest that the caller re-dial since he probably dialed incorrectly
    D. tell the caller he has reached the wrong office and then hang up

    2._____

3. When you answer the telephone, the MOST important reason for identifying yourself and your organization is to

    A. give the caller time to collect his or her thoughts
    B. impress the caller with your courtesy
    C. inform the caller that he or she has reached the right number
    D. set a business-like tone at the beginning of the conversation

    3._____

4. The one of the following cases in which you would NOT place a special notation in the left margin of a letter that you have typed is when

    A. one of the copies is intended for someone other than the addressee of the letter
    B. you enclose a flyer with the letter
    C. you sign your superior's name to the letter, at his or her request
    D. the letter refers to something being sent under separate cover

    4._____

5. Suppose that you accidentally cut a letter or enclosure as you are opening an envelope with a paper knife.
The one of the following that you should do FIRST is to

    A. determine whether the document is important
    B. clip or staple the pieces together and process as usual
    C. mend the cut document with transparent tape
    D. notify the sender that the communication was damaged and request another copy

    5._____

19

6. As soon as you pick up the phone, a very angry caller begins immediately to complain about city agencies and *red tape*. He says that he has been shifted to two or three different offices. It turns out that he is seeking information which is not immediately available to you. You believe you know, however, where it can be found.
Which of the following actions is the BEST one for you to take?

    A. To eliminate all confusion, suggest that the caller write the mayor stating explicitly what he wants.
    B. Apologize by telling the caller how busy city agencies now are, but also tell him directly that you do not have the information he needs.
    C. Ask for the caller's telephone number, and assure him you will call back after you have checked further.
    D. Give the caller the name and telephone number of the person who might be able to help, but explain that you are not positive he will get results.

7. Suppose that one of your duties is to dictate responses to routine requests from the public for information. A letter writer asks for information which, as expressed in a one-sentence, explicit agency rule, cannot be given out to the public.
Of the following ways of answering the letter, which is the MOST efficient?

    A. Quote verbatim that section of the agency rules which prohibits giving this information to the public.
    B. Without quoting the rule, explain why you cannot accede to the request and suggest alternative sources.
    C. Describe how carefully the request was considered before classifying it as subject to the rule forbidding the issuance of such information.
    D. Acknowledge receipt of the letter and advise that the requested information is not released to the public.

8. Suppose you assist in supervising a staff which has rather high morale, and your own supervisor asks you to poll the staff to find out who will be able to work overtime this particular evening to help complete emergency work.
Which of the following approaches would be MOST likely to win their cooperation while maintaining their morale?

    A. Tell them that the better assignments will be given only to those who work overtime.
    B. Tell them that occasional overtime is a job requirement.
    C. Assure them they'll be doing you a personal favor.
    D. Let them know clearly why the overtime is needed.

9. Suppose that you have been asked to write and to prepare for reproduction new departmental vacation leave regulations.
After you have written the new regulations, all of which fit on two pages, which one of the following would be the BEST method of reproducing 1,000 copies?

    A. An outside private printer because you can best maintain confidentiality using this technique
    B. Photocopying because the copies will have the best possible appearance
    C. Sending the file to all department employees as printable PDFs
    D. Printing and collating on the office high-volume printer

10. You are in charge of verifying employees' qualifications. This involves telephoning previous employers and schools. One of the applications which you are reviewing contains information which you are almost certain is correct on the basis of what the employee has told you.
    The BEST thing to do is to

    A. check the information again with the employer
    B. perform the required verification procedures
    C. accept the information as valid
    D. ask a superior to verify the information

11. The practice of immediately identifying oneself and one's place of employment when contacting persons on the telephone is

    A. *good* because the receiver of the call can quickly identify the caller and establish a frame of reference
    B. *good* because it helps to set the caller at ease with the other party
    C. *poor* because it is not necessary to divulge that information when making general calls
    D. *poor* because it takes longer to arrive at the topic to be discussed

12. Which one of the following should be the MOST important overall consideration when preparing a recommendation to automate a large-scale office activity?
    The

    A. number of models of automated equipment available
    B. benefits and costs of automation
    C. fears and resistance of affected employees
    D. experience of offices which have automated similar activities

13. A tickler file is MOST appropriate for filing materials

    A. chronologically according to date they were received
    B. alphabetically by name
    C. alphabetically by subject
    D. chronologically according to date they should be followed up

14. Which of the following is the BEST reason for decentralizing rather then centralizing the use of duplicating machines?

    A. Developing and retaining efficient duplicating machine operators
    B. Facilitating supervision of duplicating services
    C. Motivating employees to produce legible duplicated copies
    D. Placing the duplicating machines where they are most convenient and most frequently used

15. Window envelopes are sometimes considered preferable to individually addressed envelopes PRIMARILY because

    A. window envelopes are available in standard sizes for all purposes
    B. window envelopes are more attractive and official-looking
    C. the use of window envelopes eliminates the risk of inserting a letter in the wrong envelope
    D. the use of window envelopes requires neater typing

16. In planning the layout of a new office, the utilization of space and the arrangement of staff, furnishings, and equipment should usually be MOST influenced by the

    A. gross square footage
    B. status differences in the chain of command
    C. framework of informal relationships among employees
    D. activities to be performed

17. Office forms sometimes consist of several copies, each of a different color. The MAIN reason for using different colors is to

    A. make a favorable impression on the users of the form
    B. distinguish each copy from the others
    C. facilitate the preparation of legible carbon copies
    D. reduce cost, since using colored stock permits recycling of paper

18. Which of the following is the BEST justification for obtaining a photocopying machine for the office?

    A. A photocopying machine can produce an unlimited number of copies at a low fixed cost per copy.
    B. Employees need little training in operating a photocopying machine.
    C. Office costs will be reduced and efficiency increased.
    D. The legibility of a photocopy generally is superior to copy produced by any other office duplicating device.

19. An administrative officer in charge of a small fund for buying office supplies has just written a check to Charles Laird, a supplier, and has sent the check by messenger to him. A half-hour later, the messenger telephones the administrative officer. He has lost the check.
    Which of the following is the MOST important action for the administrative officer to take under these circumstances?

    A. Ask the messenger to return and write a report describing the loss of the check.
    B. Make a note on the performance record of the messenger who lost the check.
    C. Take the necessary steps to have payment stopped on the check.
    D. Refrain from doing anything since the check may be found shortly.

20. A petty cash fund is set up PRIMARILY to

    A. take care of small investments that must be made from time to time
    B. take care of small expenses that arise from time to time
    C. provide a fund to be used as the office wants to use it with little need to maintain records
    D. take care of expenses that develop during emergencies such as machine breakdowns and fires

21. Your superior has asked you to send a package from your agency to a government agency in another city. He has written out the message and has indicated the name of the government agency.
    When you prepare the package for mailing, which of the following items that your superior has not mentioned must you be sure to include?

A. Today's date
B. The full address of the government agency
C. A polite opening such as *Dear Sirs*
D. A final sentence such as *We would appreciate hearing from your agency in reply as soon as is convenient for you*

22. In addition to the original piece of correspondence, one should USUALLY also have typed

    A. a single copy
    B. as many copies as can be typed at one time
    C. no more copies than are needed
    D. two copies

22.____

23. The one of the following which is the BEST procedure to follow when making a short insert in a completed dictation is to

    A. label the insert with a letter and indicate the position of the insert in the text by writing the identifying letter in the proper place
    B. squeeze the insert into its proper place within the main text of the dictation
    C. take down the insert and check the placement with the person who dictated when you are ready to transcribe your notes
    D. transcribe the dictation into longhand, including the insert in its proper position

23.____

24. The one of the following procedures which will be MOST efficient in helping you to quickly open your dictation notebook to a clean sheet is to

    A. clip or place a rubberband around the used portion of the notebook
    B. leave the book out and open to a clean page when not in use
    C. transcribe each dictation after it is given and rip out the used pages
    D. use a book marker to indicate which portion of the notebook has been used

24.____

25. The purpose of dating your dictation notebooks is GENERALLY to

    A. enable you to easily refer to your notes at a later date
    B. ensure that you transcribe your notes in the order in which they were dictated
    C. set up a precise record-keeping procedure
    D. show your employer that you pay attention to detail

25.____

KEY (CORRECT ANSWERS)

1. C
2. B
3. C
4. C
5. C

6. C
7. A
8. D
9. D
10. B

11. A
12. B
13. D
14. D
15. C

16. D
17. B
18. C
19. C
20. B

21. B
22. C
23. A
24. A
25. A

———

TEST 2

DIRECTIONS: Each question or incomplete statement is followed by several suggested answers or completions. Select the one that BEST answers the question or completes the statement. *PRINT THE LETTER OF THE CORRECT ANSWER IN THE SPACE AT THE RIGHT.*

1. With regard to typed correspondence received by most offices, which of the following is the GREATEST problem?   1._____

    A. Verbosity
    B. Illegibility
    C. Improper folding
    D. Excessive copies

2. Of the following, the GREATEST advantage of flash drives over rewritable CD storage is that they   2._____

    A. are portable
    B. are both smaller and lighter
    C. contain more storage space
    D. allow files to be deleted to free space

3. Suppose that a large quantity of information is in the files which are located a good distance from your desk. Almost every worker in your office must use these files constantly. Your duties in particular require that you daily refer to about 25 of the same items. They are short, one-page items distributed throughout the files. In this situation, your BEST course would be to   3._____

    A. take the items that you use daily from the files and keep them on your desk, inserting *out cards* in their place
    B. go to the files each time you need the information so that the items will be there when other workers need them
    C. make xerox copies of the information you use most frequently and keep them in your desk for ready reference
    D. label the items you use most often with different colored tabs for immediate identification

4. Of the following, the MOST important advantage of preparing manuals of office procedures in loose-leaf form is that this form   4._____

    A. permits several employees to use different sections simultaneously
    B. facilitates the addition of new material and the removal of obsolete material
    C. is more readily arranged in alphabetical order
    D. reduces the need for cross-references to locate material carried under several headings

5. Suppose that you establish a new clerical procedure for the unit you supervise. Your keeping a close check on the time required by your staff to handle the new procedure is WISE mainly because such a check will find out   5._____

    A. whether your subordinates know how to handle the new procedure
    B. whether a revision of the unit's work schedule will be necessary as a result of the new procedure
    C. what attitude your employees have toward the new procedure
    D. what alterations in job descriptions will be necessitated by the new procedure

6. The numbered statements below relate to the stenographic skill of taking dictation. According to authorities on secretarial practices, which of these are generally recommended guides to development of efficient stenographic skills?

STATEMENTS
1. A stenographer should date her notebook daily to facilitate locating certain notes at a later time.
2. A stenographer should make corrections of grammatical mistakes while her boss is dictating to her.
3. A stenographer should draw a line through the dictated matter in her notebook after she has transcribed it.
4. A stenographer should write in longhand unfamiliar names and addresses dictated to her.

The CORRECT answer is:

A. Only Statements 1, 2, and 3 are generally recommended guides.
B. Only Statements 2, 3, and 4 are generally recommended guides.
C. Only Statements 1, 3, and 4 are generally recommended guides.
D. All four statements are generally recommended guides.

7. According to generally recognized rules of filing in an alphabetic filing system, the one of the following names which normally should be filed LAST is

A. Department of Education, New York State
B. F.B.I.
C. Police Department of New York City
D. P.S. 81 of New York City

8. Which one of the following forms for the typed name of the dictator in the closing lines of a letter is generally MOST acceptable in the United States?

A. (Dr.) James F. Fenton
B. Dr. James F. Fenton
C. Mr. James F. Fenton, Ph.D.
D. James F. Fenton

9. Which of the following is, MOST generally, a rule to be followed when typing a rough draft?

A. The copy should be single spaced.
B. The copy should be triple spaced.
C. There is no need for including footnotes.
D. Errors must be neatly corrected.

10. An office assistant needs a synonym.
Of the following, the book which she would find MOST useful is

A. a world atlas
B. BARTLETT'S FAMILIAR QUOTATIONS
C. a manual of style
D. a thesaurus

11. Of the following examples of footnotes, the one that is expressed in the MOST generally accepted standard form is: 11.____

    A. Johnson, T.F. (Dr.), <u>English for Everyone</u>, 3rd or 4th edition; New York City Linton Publishing Company, p. 467
    B. Frank Taylor, <u>English for Today</u> (New York: Rayton Publishing Company, 1971), p. 156
    C. Ralph Wilden, <u>English for Tomorrow,</u> Reynolds Publishing Company, England, p. 451
    D. Quinn, David, Yesterday's English (New York: Baldwin Publishing Company, 1972), p. 431

12. Standard procedures are used in offices PRIMARILY because 12.____

    A. an office is a happier place if everyone is doing the tasks in the same manner
    B. particular ways of doing jobs are considered more efficient than other ways
    C. it is good discipline for workers to follow standard procedures approved by the supervisor
    D. supervisors generally don't want workers to be creative in planning their work

13. Assume that an office assistant has the responsibility for compiling, typing, and mailing a preliminary announcement of Spring term course offerings. The announcement will go to approximately 900 currently enrolled students. Assuming that the following equipment is available for use, the MOST EFFECTIVE method for distributing the announcement to all 900 students is to 13.____

    A. e-mail it as a text document using the electronic student mailing list
    B. post the announcement as a PDF document for download on the department website
    C. send it by fax
    D. post the announcement and leave copies in buildings around campus

14. *Justified typing* is a term that refers MOST specifically to typewriting copy 14.____

    A. that has been edited and for which final copy is being prepared
    B. in a form that allows for an even right-hand margin
    C. with a predetermined vertical placement for each alternate line
    D. that has been approved by the supervisor and his superior

15. Which one of the following is the BEST form for the address in a letter? 15.____

    A. Mr. John Jones
       Vice President, The Universal Printing Company
       1220 Fifth Avenue
       New York, 10023 New York
    B. Mr. John Jones, Vice President
       The Universal Printing Company
       1220 Fifth Avenue
       New York, New York 10023
    C. Mr. John Jones, Vice President, The Universal Printing Company
       1220 Fifth Avenue
       New York, New York 10023

D. Mr. John Jones Vice President,
The Universal Printing Company
1220 Fifth Avenue
New York, 10023 New York

16. Of the following, the CHIEF advantage of the use of window envelopes over ordinary envelopes is that window envelopes

    A. eliminate the need for addressing envelopes
    B. protect the confidential nature of enclosed material
    C. cost less to buy than ordinary envelopes
    D. reduce the danger of the address becoming illegible

17. In the complimentary close of a business letter, the FIRST letter of _____ should be capitalized.

    A. all the words
    B. none of the words
    C. only the first word
    D. only the last word

18. Assume that one of your duties is to procure needed office supplies from the supply room. You are permitted to draw supplies every two weeks.
    The one of the following which would be the MOST desirable practice for you to follow in obtaining supplies is to

    A. obtain a quantity of supplies sufficient to last for several months to make certain that enough supplies are always on hand
    B. determine the minimum supply necessary to keep on hand for the various items and obtain an additional quantity as soon as possible after the supply on hand has been reduced to this minimum
    C. review the supplies once a month to determine what items have been exhausted and obtain an additional quantity as soon as possible
    D. obtain a supply of an item as soon after it has been exhausted as is possible

19. Some offices that keep carbon copies of letters use several different colors of carbon paper for making carbon copies.
    Of the following, the CHIEF reason for using different colors of carbon paper is to

    A. facilitate identification of different types of letters in the files
    B. relieve the monotony of typing and filing carbon copies
    C. reduce the costs of preparing carbon copies
    D. utilize both sides of the carbon paper for typing

20. Your supervisor asks you to post an online ad for freelance designers interested in submitting samples for a new company logo. Prospective workers should be proficient in which of the following software?

    A. Microsoft Word
    B. Adobe Acrobat Pro
    C. Adobe Illustrator
    D. Microsoft PowerPoint

21. Gary Thompson is applying for a position with the firm of Gray and Williams.
    Which letter should be filed in top position in the *Application* folder?

    A. A letter of recommendation written on September 18 by Johnson & Smith
    B. Williams' letter of October 8 requesting further details regarding Thompson's experience

C. Thompson's letter of September 8 making application for a position as sales manager
D. Letter of September 20 from Alfred Jackson recommending Thompson for the job

22. The USUAL arrangement in indexing the names of the First National Bank, Toledo, is   22.____

    A. First National Bank, Toledo, Ohio
    B. Ohio, First National Bank, Toledo
    C. Toledo, First National Bank, Ohio
    D. Ohio, Toledo, First National Bank

23. A single line through typed text indicating that it's incorrect or invalid is known as a(n)   23.____

    A. underline
    B. strikethrough
    C. line font
    D. eraser

24. A typical e-mail with an attachment should contain all of the following for successful transmittal EXCEPT   24.____

    A. recipient's address   B. file attachment
    C. body text   D. description of attachment

25. The subject line in a letter is USUALLY typed a _____ space below the _____.   25.____

    A. single; inside address   B. single; salutation
    C. double; inside address   D. double; salutation

KEY (CORRECT ANSWERS)

1. A		11. B	
2. C		12. B	
3. C		13. A	
4. B		14. B	
5. B		15. B	
6. C		16. A	
7. D		17. C	
8. D		18. B	
9. B		19. A	
10. D		20. C	

21. B
22. A
23. B
24. D
25. D

SPELLING

EXAMINATION SECTION

TEST 1

DIRECTIONS: Each question or incomplete statement is followed by several suggested answers or completions. Select the one that BEST answers the question or completes the statement. *PRINT THE LETTER OF THE CORRECT ANSWER IN THE SPACE AT THE RIGHT.*

Questions 1-5.

DIRECTIONS: Questions 1 through 5 consist of four words. Indicate the letter of the word that is CORRECTLY spelled.

1. A. harassment B. harrasment 1.____
   C. harasment D. harrassment

2. A. maintainance B. maintenence 2.____
   C. maintainence D. maintenance

3. A. comparable B. comprable 3.____
   C. comparible D. commparable

4. A. suficient B. sufficant 4.____
   C. sufficient D. suficiant

5. A. fairly B. fairley C. farely D. fairlie 5.____

Questions 6-10.

DIRECTIONS: Questions 6 through 10 consist of four words. Indicate the letter of the word that is INCORRECTLY spelled.

6. A. pallor B. ballid C. ballet D. pallid 6.____

7. A. urbane B. surburbane 7.____
   C. interurban D. urban

8. A. facial B. physical C. fiscle D. muscle 8.____

9. A. interceed B. benefited 9.____
   C. analogous D. altogether

10. A. seizure B. irrelevant 10.____
    C. inordinate D. dissapproved

31

KEY (CORRECT ANSWERS)

1. A
2. D
3. A
4. C
5. A
6. B
7. B
8. C
9. A
10. D

TEST 2

DIRECTIONS: Each of Questions 1 through 15 consists of two words preceded by the letters A and B. In each question, one of the words may be spelled INCORRECTLY or both words may be spelled CORRECTLY. If one of the words in a question is spelled INCORRECTLY, print in the space at the right the capital letter preceding the INCORRECTLY spelled word. If both words are spelled CORRECTLY, print the letter C.

1. A. easely   B. readily   1.____
2. A. pursue   B. decend   2.____
3. A. measure   B. laboratory   3.____
4. A. exausted   B. traffic   4.____
5. A. discussion   B. unpleasant   5.____
6. A. campaign   B. murmer   6.____
7. A. guarantee   B. sanatary   7.____
8. A. communication B. safty   8.____
9. A. numerus   B. celebration   9.____
10. A. nourish   B. begining   10.____
11. A. courious   B. witness   11.____
12. A. undoubtedly   B. thoroughly   12.____
13. A. accessible   B. artifical   13.____
14. A. feild   B. arranged   14.____
15. A. admittence   B. hastily   15.____

KEY (CORRECT ANSWERS)

1.	A	6.	B	11.	A
2.	B	7.	B	12.	C
3.	C	8.	B	13.	B
4.	A	9.	A	14.	A
5.	C	10.	B	15.	A

TEST 3

DIRECTIONS: In each of the following sentences, one word is misspelled. Following each sentence is a list of four words taken from the sentence. Indicate the letter of the word which is MISSPELLED in the sentence. *PRINT THE LETTER OF THE CORRECT ANSWER IN THE SPACE AT THE RIGHT.*

1. The placing of any inflammable substance in any building, or the placing of any device or contrivance capable of producing fire, for the purpose of causing a fire is an attempt to burn.
   A. inflammable
   B. substance
   C. device
   D. contrivence

   1.____

2. The word *break* also means obtaining an entrance into a building by any artifice used for that purpose, or by collussion with any person therein.
   A. obtaining
   B. entrance
   C. artifice
   D. colussion

   2.____

3. Any person who with intent to provoke a breech of the peace causes a disturbance or is offensive to others may be deemed to have committed disorderly conduct.
   A. breech
   B. disturbance
   C. offensive
   D. committed

   3.____

4. When the offender inflicts a grevious harm upon the person from whose possession, or in whose presence, property is taken, he is guilty of robbery.
   A. offender
   B. grevious
   C. possession
   D. presence

   4.____

5. A person who wilfuly encourages or advises another person in attempting to take the latter's life is guilty of a felony.
   A. wilfuly
   B. encourages
   C. advises
   D. attempting

   5.____

6. He maliciously demurred to an ajournment of the proceedings.
   A. maliciously
   B. demurred
   C. ajournment
   D. proceedings

   6.____

7. His innocence at that time is irrelevant in view of his more recent villianous demeanor.
   A. innocence
   B. irrelevant
   C. villianous
   D. demeanor

   7.____

8. The mischievous boys aggrevated the annoyance of their neighbor.
   A. mischievous
   B. aggrevated
   C. annoyance
   D. neighbor

   8.____

9. While his perseverence was commendable, his judgment was debatable. 9.____
   A. perseverence B. commendable
   C. judgment D. debatable

10. He was hoping the appeal would facilitate his aquittal. 10.____
    A. hoping B. appeal
    C. facilitate D. aquittal

11. It would be preferable for them to persue separate courses. 11.____
    A. preferable B. persue
    C. separate D. courses

12. The litigant was complimented on his persistance and achievement. 12.____
    A. litigant B. complimented
    C. persistance D. achievement

13. Ocassionally there are discrepancies in the descriptions of miscellaneous items. 13.____
    A. ocassionally B. discrepancies
    C. descriptions D. miscellaneous

14. The councilmanic seargent-at-arms enforced the prohibition. 14.____
    A. councilmanic B. seargeant-at-arms
    C. enforced D. prohibition

15. The teacher had an ingenious device for maintaining attendance. 15.____
    A. ingenious B. device
    C. maintaning D. attendance

16. A worrysome situation has developed as a result of the assessment that absenteeism is increasing despite our conscientious efforts. 16.____
    A. worrysome B. assessment
    C. absenteeism D. conscientious

17. I concurred with the credit manager that it was practicable to charge purchases on a biennial basis, and the company agreed to adhear to this policy. 17.____
    A. concurred B. practicable
    C. biennial D. adhear

18. The pastor was chagrined and embarassed by the irreverent conduct of one of his parishioners. 18.____
    A. chagrined B. embarassed
    C. irreverent D. parishioners

19. His inate seriousness was belied by his flippant demeanor. 19.____
    A. inate B. belied
    C. flippant D. demeanor

20. It was exceedingly regrettable that the excessive number of challenges in the court delayed the start of the trial.
    A. exceedingly
    B. regrettable
    C. excessive
    D. challanges

20._____

KEY (CORRECT ANSWERS)

1.	D	11.	B
2.	D	12.	C
3.	A	13.	A
4.	B	14.	B
5.	A	15.	C
6.	C	16.	A
7.	C	17.	D
8.	B	18.	B
9.	A	19.	A
10.	D	20.	D

TEST 4

Questions 1-11.

DIRECTIONS: Each question consists of three words in each question, one of the words may be spelled incorrectly or all three may be spelled correctly. For each question if one of the words is spelled INCORRECTLY, write the letter of the incorrect word in the space at the right. If all three words are spelled CORRECTLY, write the letter D in the space at the right.

SAMPLE I: (A) guide   (B) departmint   (C) stranger
SAMPLE II: (A) comply   (B) valuable   (C) window
In Sample I, departmint is incorrect. It should be spelled department.
Therefore, B is the answer.
In Sample II, all three words are spelled correctly. Therefore, D is the answer.

1. A. argument   B. reciept   C. complain   1.____
2. A. sufficient   B. postpone   C. visible   2.____
3. A. expirience   B. dissatisly   C. alternate   3.____
4. A. occurred   B. noticable   C. appendix   4.____
5. A. anxious   B. guarantee   C. calendar   5.____
6. A. sincerely   B. affectionately   C. truly   6.____
7. A. excellant   B. verify   C. important   7.____
8. A. error   B. quality   C. enviroment   8.____
9. A. exercise   B. advance   C. pressure   9.____
10. A. citizen   B. expence   C. memory   10.____
11. A. flexable   B. focus   C. forward   11.____

Questions 12-15.

DIRECTIONS: Each of Questions 12 through 15 consists of a group of four words. Examine each group carefully; then in the space at the right, indicate
   A. if only one word in the group is spelled correctly
   B. if two words in the group are spelled correctly
   C. if three words in the group are spelled correctly
   D. if all four words in the group are spelled correctly

12. Wendsday, particular, similar, hunderd   12.____

13. realize, judgment, opportunities, consistent   13.____

14. equel, principle, assistense, committee   14.____

15. simultaneous, privilege, advise, ocassionaly   15.____

KEY (CORRECT ANSWERS)

1.	B	6.	D	11.	A
2.	D	7.	A	12.	B
3.	A	8.	C	13.	D
4.	B	9.	D	14.	A
5.	C	10.	B	15.	C

TEST 5

DIRECTIONS: Each of Questions 1 through 15 consists of two words preceded by the letters A and B. In each item, one of the words may be spelled INCORRECTLY or both words may be spelled CORRECTLY. If one of the words in a question is spelled INCORRECTLY, print in the space at the right the letter preceding the INCORRECTLY spelled word. If bot words are spelled CORRECTLY, print the letter C.

1. A. justified B. offering 1.____
2. A. predjudice B. license 2.____
3. A. label B. pamphlet 3.____
4. A. bulletin B. physical 4.____
5. A. assure B. exceed 5.____
6. A. advantagous B. evident 6.____
7. A. benefit B. occured 7.____
8. A. acquire B. graditude 8.____
9. A. amenable B. boundry 9.____
10. A. deceive B. voluntary 10.____
11. A. imunity B. conciliate 11.____
12. A. acknoledge B. presume 12.____
13. A. substitute B. prespiration 13.____
14. A. reputable B. announce 14.____
15. A. luncheon B. wretched 15.____

KEY (CORRECT ANSWERS)

1.	C	6.	A	11.	A
2.	A	7.	B	12.	A
3.	C	8.	B	13.	B
4.	C	9.	B	14.	A
5.	C	10.	C	15.	C

TEST 6

DIRECTIONS: Questions 1 through 15 contain lists of words, one of which is misspelled. Indicate the MISSPELLED word in each group. *PRINT THE LETTER OF THE CORRECT ANSWER IN THE SPACE AT THE RIGHT.*

1. A. felony   B. lacerate   1.____
   C. cancellation   D. seperate

2. A. batallion   B. beneficial   2.____
   C. miscellaneous   D. secretary

3. A. camouflage   B. changeable   3.____
   C. embarrass   D. inoculate

4. A. beneficial   B. disasterous   4.____
   C. incredible   D. miniature

5. A. auxilliary   B. hypocrisy   5.____
   C. phlegm   D. vengeance

6. A. aisle   B. cemetary   6.____
   C. courtesy   D. extraordinary

7. A. crystallize   B. innoculate   7.____
   C. eminent   D. symmetrical

8. A. judgment   B. maintainance   8.____
   C. bouillon   D. cory

9. A. isosceles   B. ukulele   9.____
   C. mayonaise   D. iridescent

10. A. remembrance   B. occurence   10.____
    C. correspondence D. countenance

11. A. corpuscles   B. mischievous   11.____
    C. batchelor   D. bulletin

12. A. terrace   B. banister   12.____
    C. concrete   D. masonery

13. A. balluster   B. gutter   13.____
    C. latch   D. bridging

14. A. personnell   B. navel   14.____
    C. therefor   D. emigrant

15. A. committee B. submiting
    C. amendment D. electorate   15._____

KEY (CORRECT ANSWERS)

1. D   6. B   11. C
2. A   7. B   12. D
3. C   8. B   13. A
4. B   9. C   14. A
5. A   10. B   15. B

TEST 7

Questions 1-5.

DIRECTIONS: Questions 1 through 5 consist of groups of four words. Select answer
A if only one word is spelled correctly in a group
B if TWO words are spelled correctly in a group
C if THREE words are spelled correctly in a group
D if all FOUR words are spelled correctly in a group.

1. counterfeit,   embarass,   panicky,   supercede   1._____

2. benefited,   personnel,   questionnaire,   unparalelled   2._____

3. bankruptcy,   describable,   proceed,   vacuum   3._____

4. handicapped,   mispell,   offerred,   pilgrimmage   4._____

5. corduroy,   interfere,   privilege,   separator   5._____

Questions 6-10.

DIRECTIONS: Questions 6 through 10 consist of four pairs of words each. Some of the words are spelled correctly; others are spelled incorrectly. For each question, indicate in the space at the right the letter preceding that pair of words in which BOTH words are spelled CORRECTLY.

6. A. hygienic, inviegle   B. omniscience, pittance   6._____
    C. plagarize, nullify   D. scargent, perilous

7. A. auxilary, existence   B. pronounciation, accordance 7._____
    C. ignominy, indegence   D. suable, baccalaureate

8. A. discreet, inaudible   B. hypocrisy, currupt   8._____
    C. liquidate, maintainance   D. transparancy, onerous

9. A. facility; stimulent   B. frugel, sanitary   9._____
    C. monetary, prefatory   D. punctileous, credentials

10. A. bankruptsy, perceptible   B. disuade, resilient   10._____
    C. exhilerate, expectancy   D. panegyric, disparate

Questions 11-15.

DIRECTIONS: Each question or incomplete statement is followed by several suggested answers or completions. Select the one that BEST answers the question or completes the statement. PRINT THE LETTER OF THE CORRECT ANSWER IN THE SPACE AT THE RIGHT.

11. The silent *e* must be retained when the suffix *–able* is added to the word 11._____
    A. argue   B. love   C. move   D. notice

12. The CORRECTLY spelled word in the choices below is 12._____
    A. kindergarden   B. zylophone
    C. hemorrhage   D. mayonaise

13. Of the following words, the one spelled CORRECTLY is 13._____
    A. begger   B. cemetary
    C. embarassed   D. coyote

14.   A. dandilion   B. wiry   C. sieze   D. rythmic 14._____

15.   A. beligerent   B. anihilation
    C. facetious   D. adversery

KEY (CORRECT ANSWERS)

1.	B	6.	B	11.	D
2.	C	7.	D	12.	C
3.	D	8.	A	13.	D
4.	A	9.	C	14.	B
5.	D	10.	D	15.	C

TEST 8

DIRECTIONS: In each of the following sentences, one word is misspelled. Following each sentence is a list of four words taken from the sentence. Indicate the letter of the word which is MISSPELLED. *PRINT THE LETTER OF THE CORRECT ANSWER IN THE SPACE AT THE RIGHT.*

1. If the administrator attempts to withold information, there is a good likelihood that there will be serious repercussions.
    A. administrator
    B. withold
    C. likelihood
    D. repercussions

2. He condescended to apologize, but we felt that a beligerent person should not occupy an influential position.
    A. condescended
    B. apologize
    C. beligerent
    D. influential

3. Despite the sporadic delinquent payments of his indebtedness, Mr. Johnson has been an exemplery customer.
    A. sporadic
    B. delinquent
    C. indebtedness
    D. exemplery

4. He was appreciative of the support he consistantly acquired, but he felt that he had waited an inordinate length of time for it.
    A. appreciative
    B. consistantly
    C. acquired
    D. inordinate

5. Undeniably they benefited from the establishment of a receivership, but the question of statutary limitations remained unresolved.
    A. undeniably
    B. benefited
    C. receivership
    D. statutary

6. Mr. Smith profered his hand as an indication that he considered it a viable contract, but Mr. Nelson alluded to the fact that his colleagues had not been consulted.
    A. profered
    B. viable
    C. alluded
    D. colleagues

7. The treatments were beneficial according to the optomotrists, and the consensus was that minimal improvement could be expected.
    A. beneficial
    B. optomotrists
    C. consensus
    D. minimal

8. Her frivolous manner was unbecoming because the air of solemnity at the cemetery was pervasive.
    A. frivalous
    B. solemnity
    C. cemetery
    D. pervasive

9. The clandestine meetings were designed to make the two adversaries more amicable, but they served only to intensify their emnity.
   A. clandestine
   B. adversaries
   C. amicable
   D. emnity

   9.____

10. Do you think that his innovative ideas and financial acumen will help stabalize the fluctuations of the stock market?
    A. innovative
    B. acumen
    C. stabalize
    D. fluctuations

    10.____

11. In order to keep a perpetual inventory, you will have to keep an uninterrupted surveillance of all the miscellanious stock.
    A. perpetual
    B. uninterrupted
    C. surveillance
    D. miscellanious

    11.____

12. She used the art of pursuasion on the children because she found that caustic remarks had no perceptible effect on their behavior.
    A. pursuasion
    B. caustic
    C. perceptible
    D. effect

    12.____

13. His sacreligious outbursts offended his constituents, and he was summarily removed from office by the City Council.
    A. sacreligious
    B. constituents
    C. summarily
    D. Council

    13.____

14. They exhorted the contestants to greater efforts, but the exhorbitant costs in terms of energy expended resulted in a feeling of lethargy.
    A. exhorted
    B. contestants
    C. exhorbitant
    D. lethargy

    14.____

15. Since he was knowledgable about illicit drugs, he was served with a subpoena to appear for the prosecution.
    A. knowledgable
    B. illicit
    C. subpoena
    D. prosecution

    15.____

16. In spite of his lucid statements, they denigrated his report and decided it should be succintly paraphrased.
    A. lucid
    B. denigrated
    C. succintly
    D. paraphrased

    16.____

17. The discussion was not germane to the contraversy, but the indicted man's insistence on further talk was allowed.
    A. germane
    B. contraversy
    C. indicted
    D. insistence

    17.____

18. The legislators were enervated by the distances they had traveled during the election year to fullfil their speaking engagements.
    A. legislators
    B. enervated
    C. traveled
    D. fullfil

    18.____

19. The plaintiffs' attornies charge the defendant in the case with felonious assault.   19._____
    A. plaintiffs' B. attornies
    C. defendant   D. felonious

20. It is symptomatic of the times that we try to placate all, but a proposal for new forms of disciplinery action was promulgated by the staff.   20._____
    A. symptomatic B. placate
    C. disciplinery D. promulgated

KEY (CORRECT ANSWERS)

1.	B	11.	D
2.	C	12.	A
3.	D	13.	A
4.	B	14.	C
5.	D	15.	A
6.	A	16.	C
7.	B	17.	B
8.	A	18.	D
9.	D	19.	B
10.	C	20.	C

TEST 9

DIRECTIONS: Each of Questions 1 through 15 consists of a single word which is spelled either correctly or incorrectly. If the word is spelled CORRECTLY, you are to print the letter C (Correct) in the space at the right. If the word is spelled INCORRECTL, you are to print the letter W (Wrong).

1. pospone   1.____
2. diffrent   2.____
3. height   3.____
4. carefully   4.____
5. ability   5.____
6. temper   6.____
7. deslike   7.____
8. seldem   8.____
9. alcohol   9.____
10. expense   10.____
11. vegatable   11.____
12. dispensary   12.____
13. specemin   13.____
14. allowance   14.____
15. exersise   15.____

KEY (CORRECT ANSWERS)

1.	W	6.	C	11.	W
2.	W	7.	W	12.	C
3.	C	8.	W	13.	W
4.	C	9.	C	14.	C
5.	C	10.	C	15.	W

TEST 10

DIRECTIONS: Each of Questions 1 through 10 consists of four words, one of which may be spelled incorrectly or all four words may be spelled correctly. If one of the words in a question is spelled incorrectly, print in the space at the right the capital letter preceding the word which is spelled INCORRECTLY. If all four words are spelled CORRECTLY, print the letter E.

1. A. dismissal B. collateral 1.____
   C. leisure D. proffession

2. A. subsidary B. outrageous 2.____
   C. liaison D. assessed

3. A. already B. changeable 3.____
   C. mischevous D. cylinder

4. A. supersede B. deceit 4.____
   C. dissension D. imminent

5. A. arguing B. contagious 5.____
   C. comparitive D. accessible

6. A. indelible B. existance 6.____
   C. presumptuous D. mileage

7. A. extention B. aggregate 7.____
   C. sustenance D. gratuitous

8. A. interrogate B. exaggeration 8.____
   C. vacillate D. moreover

9. A. parallel B. derogatory 9.____
   C. admissible D. appellate

10. A. safety B. cumalative 10.____
    C. disappear D. usable

KEY (CORRECT ANSWERS)

1.	D	6.	B
2.	A	7.	A
3.	C	8.	E
4.	E	9.	C
5.	C	10.	B

TEST 11

DIRECTIONS: Each of questions 1 through 10 consists of four words, one of which may be spelled incorrectly or all four words may be spelled correctly. If one of the words in a question is spelled INCORRECTLY, print in the space at the right the capital letter preceding the word which is spelled incorrectly. If all four words are spelled CORRECTLY, print the letter E.

1. A. vehicular B. gesticulate 1.____
   C. manageable D. fullfil

2. A. inovation B. onerous 2.____
   C. chastise D. irresistible

3. A. familiarize B. dissolution 3.____
   C. oscillate D. superflous

4. A. census B. defender 4.____
   C. adherence D. inconceivable

5. A. voluminous B. liberalize 5.____
   C. bankrupcy D. conversion

6. A. justifiable B. executor 6.____
   C. perpatrate D. dispelled

7. A. boycott B. abeyence 7.____
   C. enterprise D. circular

8. A. spontaineous B. dubious 8.____
   C. analyze D. premonition

9. A. intelligible B. apparently 9.____
   C. genuine D. crucial

10. A. plentiful B. ascertain 10.____
    C. carreer D. preliminary

KEY (CORRECT ANSWERS)

1. D   6. C
2. A   7. B
3. D   8. A
4. E   9. E
5. C   10. C

TEST 12

DIRECTIONS: Each of questions 1 through 25 consists of four words, one of which may be spelled incorrectly or all four words may be spelled correctly. If one of the words in a question is spelled INCORRECTLY, print in the space at the right the capital letter preceding the word which is spelled incorrectly. If all four words are spelled CORRECTLY, print the letter E.

1. A. temporary   B. existance   1.____
   C. complimentary   D. altogether

2. A. privilege   B. changeable   2.____
   C. jeopardize   D. commitment

3. A. grievous   B. alloted   3.____
   C. outrageous   D. mortgage

4. A. tempermental   B. accommodating   4.____
   C. bookkeeping   D. panicky

5. A. auxiliary   B. indispensable   5.____
   C. ecstasy   D. fiery

6. A. dissappear   B. buoyant   6.____
   C. imminent   D. parallel

7. A. loosly   B. medicine   7.____
   C. schedule   D. defendant

8. A. endeavor   B. persuade   8.____
   C. retroactive   D. desparate

9. A. usage   B. servicable   9.____
   C. disadvantageous   D. remittance

10. A. beneficary   B. receipt   10.____
    C. excitable   D. implement

11. A. accompanying   B. intangible   11.____
    C. offered   D. movable

12. A. controlling   B. seize   12.____
    C. repetitious   D. miscellaneous

13. A. installation   B. accommodation   13.____
    C. consistant   D. illuminate

14. A. incidentaly   B. privilege   14.____
    C. apparent   D. chargeable

2 (#12)

15. A. prevalent   B. serial   15._____
    C. briefly   D. disatisfied

16. A. reciprocal B. concurrence   16._____
    C. persistence D. withold

17. A. deferred   B. suing   17._____
    C. fulfilled   D. pursuant

18. A. questionable   B. omission   18._____
    C. acknowledgment D. insistent

19. A. guarantee   B. committment   19._____
    C. mitigate   D. publicly

20. A. prerogative B. apprise   20._____
    C. extrordinary D. continual

21. A. arrogant   B. handicapped   21._____
    C. judicious   D. perennial

22. A. permissable B. deceive   22._____
    C. innumerable D. retrieve

23. A. notable   B. allegiance   23._____
    C. reimburse   D. illegal

24. A. wholly   B. disbursement   24._____
    C. hindrance   D. conciliatory

25. A. guidance   B. condemn   25._____
    C. publically D. coercion

51

KEY (CORRECT ANSWERS)

1.	B	11.	C
2.	E	12.	E
3.	B	13.	C
4.	A	14.	A
5.	E	15.	D
6.	A	16.	D
7.	A	17.	E
8.	D	18.	A
9.	B	19.	B
10.	A	20.	C

21. E
22. A
23. E
24. E
25. C

CLERICAL ABILITIES
EXAMINATION SECTION
TEST 1

DIRECTIONS: Each question or incomplete statement is followed by several suggested answers or completions. Select the one that BEST answers the question or completes the statement. *PRINT THE LETTER OF THE CORRECT ANSWER IN THE SPACE AT THE RIGHT.*

Questions 1-4.

DIRECTIONS: Questions 1 through 4 are to be answered on the basis of the information given below.

    The most commonly used filing system and the one that is easiest to learn is alphabetical filing. This involves putting records in an A to Z order, according to the letters of the alphabet. The name of a person is filed by using the following order: first, the surname or last name; second, the first name; third, the middle name or middle initial. For example, *Henry C. Young* is filed under *Y* and thereafter under *Young, Henry C.* The name of a company is filed in the same way. For example, *Long Cabinet Co.* is filed under *L* while *John T. Long Cabinet Co.* is filed under *L* and thereafter under *Long, John T. Cabinet Co.*

1. The one of the following which lists the names of persons in the CORRECT alphabetical order is:
    A. Mary Carrie, Helen Carrol, James Carson, John Carter
    B. James Carson, Mary Carrie, John Carter, Helen Carrol
    C. Helen Carrol, James Carson, John Carter, Mary Carrie
    D. John Carter, Helen Carrol, Mary Carrie, James Carson

1.____

2. The one of the following which lists the names of persons in the CORRECT alphabetical order is:
    A. Jones, John C.; Jones, John A.; Jones, John P.; Jones, John K.
    B. Jones, John P.; Jones, John K.; Jones, John C.; Jones, John A.
    C. Jones, John A.; Jones, John C.; Jones, John K.; Jones, John P.
    D. Jones, John K.; Jones, John C.; Jones, John A.; Jones, John P.

2.____

3. The one of the following which lists the names of the companies in the CORRECT alphabetical order is:
    A. Blane Co., Blake Co., Block Co., Blear Co.
    B. Blake Co., Blane Co., Blear Co., Block Co.
    C. Block Co., Blear Co., Blane Co., Blake Co.
    D. Blear Co., Blake Co., Blane Co., Block Co.

3.____

4. You are to return to the file an index card on *Barry C. Wayne Materials and Supplies Co.*
   Of the following, the CORRECT alphabetical group that you should return the index card to is
      A. A to G   B. H to M   C. N to S   D. T to Z

4.____

Questions 5-10.

DIRECTIONS: In each of Questions 5 through 10, the names of four people are given. For each question, choose as your answer the one of the four names given which should be filed FIRST according to the usual system of alphabetical filing of names, as described in the following paragraph.

    In filing names, you must start with the last name. Names are filed in order of the first letter of the last name, then the second letter, etc. Therefore, BAILY would be filed before BROWN, which would be filed before COLT. A name with fewer letters of the same type comes first, i.e., Smith before Smithe. If the last names are the same, the names are filed alphabetically by the first name. If the first name is an initial, a name with an initial would come before a first name that starts with the same letter as the initial. Therefore, I. BROWN would come before IRA BROWN. Finally, if both last name and first name are the same, the name would be filed alphabetically by the middle name, once again an initial coming before a middle name which starts with the same letter as the initial. If there is no middle name at all, the name would come before those with middle initials or names.

    SAMPLE QUESTION: A. Lester Daniels
                                       B. William Dancer
                                       C. Nathan Danzig
                                     D. Dan Lester

    The last names beginning with D are filed before the last name beginning with L. Since DANIELS, DANCER, and DANZIG all begin with the same three letters, you must look at the fourth letter of the last name to determine which name should be filed first. C comes before I or Z in the alphabet, so DANCER is filed before DANIELS or DANZIG. Therefore, the answer to the above sample question is B.

5.   A. Scott Biala
      B. Mary Byala
      C. Martin Baylor
      D. Francis Bauer

5.____

6.   A. Howard J. Black
      B. Howard Black
      C. J. Howard Black
      D. John H. Black

6.____

7.   A. Theodora Garth Kingston
      B. Theadore Barth Kingston
      C. Thomas Kingston
      D. Thomas T. Kingston

7.____

8. A. Paulette Mary Huerta
    B. Paul M. Huerta
    C. Paulette L. Huerta
    D. Peter A. Huerta

9. A. Martha Hunt Morgan
    B. Martin Hunt Morgan
    C. Mary H. Morgan
    D. Martine H. Morgan

10. A. James T. Meerschaum
    B. James M. Mershum
    C. James F. Mearshaum
    D. James N. Meshum

Questions 11-14.

DIRECTIONS: Questions 11 through 14 are to be answered SOLELY on the basis of the following information.

You are required to file various documents in file drawers which are labeled according to the following pattern:

DOCUMENTS

MEMOS		LETTERS	
File	Subject	File	Subject
84PM1	(A-L)	84PC1	(A-L)
84PM2	(M-Z)	84PC2	(M-Z)

REPORTS		INQUIRIES	
File	Subject	File	Subject
84PR1	(A-L)	84PQ1	(A-L)
84PR2	(M-Z)	84PQ2	(M-Z)

11. A letter dealing with a burglary should be filed in the drawer labeled
    A. 84PM1   B. 84PC1   C. 84PR1   D. 84PQ2

12. A report on Statistics should be found in the drawer labeled
    A. 84PM1   B. 84PC2   C. 84PR2   D. 84PQS

13. An inquiry is received about parade permit procedures. It should be filed in the drawer labeled
    A. 84PM2   B. 84PC1   C. 84PR1   D. 84PQ2

14. A police officer has a question about a robbery report you filed. You should pull this file from the drawer labeled
    A. 84PM1   B. 84PM2   C. 84PR1   D. 84PR2

Questions 15-22.

DIRECTIONS: Each of Questions 15 through 22 consists of four or six numbered names. For each question, choose the option (A, B, C, or D) which indicates the order in which the names should be filed in accordance with the following filing instructions:
- File alphabetically according to last name, then first name, then middle initial.
- File according to each successive letter within a name.
- When comparing two names in which the letters in the longer name are identical to the corresponding letters in the shorter name, the shorter name is filed first.
- When the last names are the same, initials are always filed before names beginning with the same letter.

15. I. Ralph Robinson
     II. Alfred Ross
     III. Luis Robles
     IV. James Roberts

    The CORRECT filing sequence for the above names should be
     A. IV, II, I, III   B. I, IV, III, II   C. III, IV, I, II   D. IV, I, III, II

16. I.   Irwin Goodwin
     II. Inez Gonzalez
     III. Irene Goodman
     IV. Ira S. Goodwin
     V.   Ruth I. Goldstein
     VI. M.B. Goodman

    The CORRECT filing sequence for the above names should be
     A. V, II, I, IV, III, VI   B. V, II, VI, III, IV, I
     C. V, II, III, VI, IV, I   D. V, II, III, VI, I, IV

17. I.   George Allan
     II. Gregory Allen
     III. Gary Allen
     IV. George Allen

    The CORRECT filing sequence for the above names should be
     A. IV, III, I, II   B. I, IV, II, III   C. III, IV, I, II   D. I, III, IV, II

18. I. Simon Kauffman
     II. Leo Kaufman
     III. Robert Kaufmann
     IV. Paul Kauffmann

   The CORRECT filing sequence for the above names should be
     A. I, IV, II, III   B. II, IV, III, I   C. III, II, IV, I   D. I, II, III, IV

19. I. Roberta Williams
     II. Robin Wilson
     III. Roberta Wilson
     IV. Robin Williams

   The CORRECT filing sequence for the above names should be
     A. III, II, IV, I   B. I, IV, III, II   C. I, II, III, IV   D. III, I, II, IV

20. I. Lawrence Shultz
     II. Albert Schultz
     III. Theodore Schwartz
     IV. Thomas Schwarz
     V. Alvin Schultz
     VI. Leonard Shultz

   The CORRECT filing sequence for the above names should be
     A. II, V, III, IV, I, VI   B. IV, III, V, I, II, VI
     C. II, V, I, VI, III, IV   D. I, VI, II, V, III, IV

21. I. McArdle
     II. Mayer
     III. Maletz
     IV. McNiff
     V. Meyer
     VI. MacMahon

   The CORRECT filing sequence for the above names should be
     A. I, IV, VI, III, II, V   B. II, I, IV, VI, III, V
     C. VI, III, II, I, IV, V   D. VI, III, II, V, I, IV

22. I. Jack E. Johnson
     II. R.H. Jackson
     III. Bertha Jackson
     IV. J.T. Johnson
     V. Ann Johns
     VI. John Jacobs

   The CORRECT filing sequence for the above names should be
     A. II, III, VI, V, IV, I   B. III, II, VI, V, IV, I
     C. VI, II, III, I, V, IV   D. III, II, VI, IV, V, I

Questions 23-30.

DIRECTIONS: The code table below shows 10 letters with matching numbers. For each question, there are three sets of letters. Each set of letters is followed by a set of numbers which may or may not match their correct letter according to the code table. For each question, check all three sets of letters and numbers and mark your answer:
    A. if no pairs are correctly matched
    B. if only one pair is correctly matched
    C. if only two pairs are correctly matched
    D. if all three pairs are correctly matched

CODE TABLE

T	M	V	D	S	P	R	G	B	H
1	2	3	4	5	6	7	8	9	0

SAMPLE QUESTION: TMVDSP – 123456
    RGBHTM – 789011
    DSPRGB – 256789

In the sample question above, the first set of numbers correctly match its set of letters. But the second and third pairs contain mistakes. In the second pair, M is correctly matched with number 1. According to the code table, letter M should be correctly matched with number 2. In the third pair, the letter D is incorrectly matched with number 2. According to the code table, letter D should be correctly matched with number 4. Since only one of the pairs is correctly matched, the answer to this sample question is B.

23.   RSBMRM – 759262
    GDSRVH – 845730
    VDBRTM - 349713

24.   TGVSDR – 183247
    SMHRDP – 520647
    TRMHSR - 172057

25.   DSPRGM – 456782
    MVDBHT – 234902
    HPMDBT - 062491

26.   BVPTRD – 936184
    GDPHMB – 807029
    GMRHMV - 827032

27.   MGVRSH – 283750
    TRDMBS – 174295
    SPRMGV - 567283

28. SGBSDM – 489542   28.____
    MGHPTM – 290612
    MPBMHT - 269301

29. TDPBHM – 146902   29.____
    VPBMRS – 369275
    GDMBHM - 842902

30. MVPTBV – 236194   30.____
    PDRTMB – 47128
    BGTMSM - 981232

KEY (CORRECT ANSWERS)

1.	A	11.	B	21.	C		
2.	C	12.	C	22.	B		
3.	B	13.	D	23.	B		
4.	D	14.	D	24.	B		
5.	D	15.	D	25.	C		
6.	B	16.	C	26.	A		
7.	B	17.	D	27.	D		
8.	B	18.	A	28.	A		
9.	A	19.	B	29.	D		
10.	C	20.	A	30.	A		

TEST 2

DIRECTIONS: Each question or incomplete statement is followed by several suggested answers or completions. Select the one that BEST answers the question or completes the statement. *PRINT THE LETTER OF THE CORRECT ANSWER IN THE SPACE AT THE RIGHT.*

Questions 1-10.

DIRECTIONS: Questions 1 through 10 each consists of two columns, each containing four lines of names, numbers and/or addresses. For each question, compare the lines in Column I with the lines in Column II to see if they match exactly, and mark your answer A, B, C, or D, according to the following instructions:
    A. all four lines match exactly
    B. only three lines match exactly
    C. only two lines match exactly
    D. only one line matches exactly

	COLUMN I	COLUMN II	
1.	I. Earl Hodgson II. 1409870 III. Shore Ave. IV. Macon Rd.	Earl Hodgson 1408970 Schore Ave. Macon Rd.	1.____
2.	I. 9671485 II. 470 Astor Court III. Halprin, Phillip IV. Frank D. Poliseo	9671485 470 Astor Court Halperin, Phillip Frank D. Poliseo	2.____
3.	I. Tandem Associates II. 144-17 Northern Blvd. III. Alberta Forchi IV. Kings Park, NY 10751	Tandom Associates 144-17 Northern Blvd. Albert Forchi Kings Point, NY 10751	3.____
4.	I. Bertha C. McCormack II. Clayton, MO III. 976-4242 IV. New City, NY 10951	Bertha C. McCormack Clayton, MO 976-4242 New City, NY 10951	4.____
5.	I. George C. Morill II. Columbia, SC 29201 III. Louis Ingham IV. 3406 Forest Ave.	George C. Morrill Columbia, SD 29201 Louis Ingham 3406 Forest Ave.	5.____
6.	I. 506 S. Elliott Pl. II. Herbert Hall III. 4712 Rockaway Pkway IV. 169 E. 7 St.	506 S. Elliott Pl. Hurbert Hall 4712 Rockaway Pkway 169 E. 7 St.	6.____

60

2 (#2)

7. I.   345 Park Ave.   345 Park Pl.   7.____
    II. Colman Oven Corp.   Coleman Oven Corp.
    III. Robert Conte   Robert Conti
    IV. 6179846   6179846

8. I.   Grigori Schierber   Grigori Schierber   8.____
    II. Des Moines, Iowa   Des Moines, Iowa
    III. Gouverneur Hospital   Gouverneur Hospital
    IV. 91-35 Cresskill Pl.   91-35 Cresskill Pl.

9. I.   Jeffery Janssen   Jeffrey Janssen   9.____
    II. 8041071   8041071
    III. 40 Rockefeller Plaza   40 Rockafeller Plaza
    IV. 407 6 St.   406 7 St.

10. I.   5971996   5871996   10.____
    II. 3113 Knickerbocker Ave.   31123 Knickerbocker Ave.
    III. 8434 Boston Post Rd.   8424 Boston Post Rd.
    IV. Penn Station   Penn Station

Questions 11-14.

DIRECTIONS: Questions 11 through 14 are to be answered by looking at the four groups of names and addresses listed below (I, II, III, and IV), and then finding out the number of groups that have their corresponding numbered lies exactly the same.

           GROUP I   GROUP II
Line 1.   Richmond General Hospital   Richman General Hospital
Line 2.   Geriatric Clinic   Geriatric Clinic
Line 3.   3975 Paerdegat St.   3975 Peardegat St.
Line 4.   Loudonville, New York 11538   Londonville, New York 11538

           GROUP III   GROUP IV
Line 1.   Richmond General Hospital   Richmend General Hospital
Line 2.   Geriatric Clinic   Geriatric Clinic
Line 3.   3795 Paerdegat St.   3975 Paerdegat St.
Line 4.   Loudonville, New York 11358   Loudonville, New York 11538

1. In how many groups is line one exactly the same?   11.____
       A. Two   B. Three   C. Four   D. None

12. In how many groups is line two exactly the same?   12.____
       A. Two   B. Three   C. Four   D. None

13. In how many groups is line three exactly the same?   13.____
       A. Two   B. Three   C. Four   D. None

14. In how many groups is line four exactly the same? 14._____
    A. Two B. Three C. Four D. None

Questions 15-18.

DIRECTIONS: Each of Questions 15 through 18 has two lists of names and addresses. Each list contains three sets of names and addresses. Check each of the three sets in the list on the right to see if they are the same as the corresponding set in the list on the left. Mark your answers:
   A. if none of the sets in the right list are the same as those in the left list
   B. if only one of the sets in the right list is the same as those in the left list
   C. if only two of the sets in the right list are the same as those in the left list
   D. if all three sets in the right list are the same as those in the left list

15. Mary T. Berlinger   Mary T. Berlinger   15._____
    2351 Hampton St.   2351 Hampton St.
    Monsey, N.Y. 20117   Monsey, N.Y. 20117

    Eduardo Benes   Eduardo Benes
    483 Kingston Avenue   473 Kingston Avenue
    Central Islip, N.Y. 11734   Central Islip, N.Y. 11734

    Alan Carrington Fuchs   Alan Carrington Fuchs
    17 Gnarled Hollow Road   17 Gnarled Hollow Road
    Los Angeles, CA 91635   Los Angeles, CA 91685

16. David John Jacobson   David John Jacobson   16._____
    178 34 St. Apt. 4C   178 53 St. Apt. 4C
    New York, N.Y. 00927   New York, N.Y. 00927

    Ann-Marie Calonella   Ann-Marie Calonella
    7243 South Ridge Blvd.   7243 South Ridge Blvd.
    Bakersfield, CA 96714   Bakersfield, CA 96714

    Pauline M. Thompson   Pauline M. Thomson
    872 Linden Ave.   872 Linden Ave.
    Houston, Texas 70321   Houston, Texas 70321

17. Chester LeRoy Masterton   Chester LeRoy Masterson   17._____
    152 Lacy Rd.   152 Lacy Rd.
    Kankakee, Ill. 54532   Kankakee, Ill. 54532

    William Maloney   William Maloney
    S. LaCrosse Pla.   S. LaCross Pla.
    Wausau, Wisconsin 52136   Wausau, Wisconsin 52146

    Cynthia V. Barnes   Cynthia V. Barnes
    16 Pines Rd.   16 Pines Rd.
    Greenpoint, Miss. 20376   Greenpoint,, Miss. 20376

18. Marcel Jean Frontenac   Marcel Jean Frontenac   18.____
    8 Burton On The Water   6 Burton On The Water
    Calender, Me. 01471   Calender, Me. 01471

    J. Scott Marsden   J. Scott Marsden
    174 S. Tipton St.   174 Tipton St.
    Cleveland, Ohio   Cleveland, Ohio

    Lawrence T. Haney   Lawrence T. Haney
    171 McDonough St.   171 McDonough St.
    Decatur, Ga. 31304   Decatur, Ga. 31304

Questions 19-26.

DIRECTIONS: Each of Questions 19 through 26 has two lists of numbers. Each list contains three sets of numbers. Check each of the three sets in the list on the right to see if they are the same as the corresponding set in the list on the left. Mark your answers:
- A. if none of the sets in the right list are the same as those in the left list
- B. if only one of the sets in the right list is the same as those in the left list
- C. if only two of the sets in the right list are the same as those in the left list
- D. if all three sets in the right list are the same as those in the left lists

19. 7354183476   7354983476   19.____
     4474747744   4474747774
     5791430231   57914302311

20. 7143592185   7143892185   20.____
     8344517699   8344518699
     9178531263   9178531263

21. 2572114731   257214731   21.____
     8806835476   8806835476
     8255831246   8255831246

22. 331476853821   331476858621   22.____
     6976658532996   6976655832996
     3766042113715   3766042113745

23. 8806663315   88066633115   23.____
     74477138449   74477138449
     211756663666   211756663666

24. 990006966996   99000696996   24.____
    53022219743   53022219843
    4171171117717   4171171177717

25. 24400222433004   24400222433004   25.____
    5300030055000355 5300030055500355
    20000075532002022 20000075532002022

26. 61116664066001116 61116664066001116 26.____
    7111300117001100733 7111300117001100733
    26666446664476518 26666446664476518

Questions 27-30.

DIRECTIONS: Questions 27 through 30 are to be answered by picking the answer which is in the correct numerical order, from the lowest number to the highest number, in each question.

27. A. 44533, 44518, 44516, 44547   27.____
     B. 44516, 44518, 44533, 44547
     C. 44547, 44533, 44518, 44516
     D. 44518, 44516, 44547, 44533

28. A. 95587, 95593, 95601, 95620   28.____
     B. 95601, 95620, 95587, 95593
     C. 95593, 95587, 95601. 95620
     D. 95620, 95601, 95593, 95587

29. A. 232212, 232208, 232232, 232223   29.____
     B. 232208, 232223, 232212, 232232
     C. 232208, 232212, 232223, 232232
     D. 232223, 232232, 232208, 232208

30. A. 113419, 113521, 113462, 113462   30.____
     B. 113588, 113462, 113521, 113419
     C. 113521, 113588, 113419, 113462
     D. 113419, 113462, 113521, 113588

KEY (CORRECT ANSWERS)

1.	C	11.	A	21.	C
2.	B	12.	C	22.	A
3.	D	13.	A	23.	D
4.	A	14.	A	24.	A
5.	C	15.	C	25.	C
6.	B	16.	B	26.	C
7.	D	17.	B	27.	B
8.	A	18.	B	28.	A
9.	D	19.	B	29.	C
10.	C	20.	B	30.	D

FILING

EXAMINATION SECTION
TEST 1

DIRECTIONS: For each of the following, you are given a name above and three other names in alphabetical order below. The letters A, B, C, and D stand for spaces where you could file the name. Find the CORRECT space for the name given above so that it will be in alphabetical order with the names below it. The letter that stands for that space is the answer to the question.

1. CURRAN, THOMAS
   A CURLEY, MARY B CURR, SAMUEL C CURREN, KATIE D

   1.____

2. KAPLIN, EDWIN
   A KAPLEN, MICHAEL B KAPLIN, JULIA C KAPLON, DAVID D

   2.____

3. PENSKY, LEONA
   A PENSLER, SANDY B PENSLEY, JOEL C PENSLEY, JOSEPH D

   3.____

4. ROWEN, MARCIA
   A ROWEN, CHRISTOPHER B ROWEN, LOUIS C ROWEN, MARTIN D

   4.____

5. FOSTER, GRACE
   A FOSS, EARL B FOSSE, NICHOLE C FOSTER, KEITH D

   5.____

6. KO, FAI
   A KO, HOK B KO, HUNG-FAI C KO, HYUN JUNG D

   6.____

7. MICHALIK, ANTHONY
   A MICHALIC, GARY B MICHALIS, HELEN C MICHALK, KLAUS D

   7.____

8. MINTZ, JUDITH
   A MINTZ, JAKE B MINTZ, JAMES C MINTZ, JULIUS D

   8.____

9. POWERS, ANN
   A POUST, THERESE B POWELL, LUTHER C POWER, RACHEL D

   9.____

10. PRACTICAL STUDIO, INC.
    A PRACTICAL PUBLISHING B PRACTICE DEVELOPMENT C PRACTICE SERVICE CORP. D

    10.____

11. SHERWIN, ROBERTA
    A SHERWIN, RAUL B SHERWIN, RICHARD C SHERWIN, ROBERT D

    11.____

12. JACOBSEN, JENNIFER
    A JACOBSON, PETER B JACOBY, JACK C JACOVITZ, GAIL D

    12.____

13. BLEINHEIM, GLORIA
    A BLELOCK, JULIA B BLENCOWE, FRED C BLENMAN, ANTHONY D

    13.____

14. FIRST STERLING CORP.
    A FIRST STATE PRODUCTS B FIRST STEP INC. C FIRST STOP CORP. D   14.____

15. VICKERS, GEORGE
    A VICHEY, LOUIS B VICHI, MARIO C VICKI, SUSAN D   15.____

16. STEIN, DAVID
    A STEIN, CRAIG B STEIN, DANIEL C STEIN, DEBORAH D   16.____

17. IGLESIAS, BERNADETTE
    A IGER, MARTIN B IGLEHEART, PHYLICIA C IGLEWSKI, RICHARD D   17.____

18. IDEAL ROOFING CORP.
    A IDEAL REPRODUCTION B IDEAL RESTAURANT C IDEAL RUBBER PRODUCTS   18.____
    D

19. TODARO, JOSEPH
    A TODD, ANNE B TODE, WALLY C TODMAN, JUDITH D   19.____

20. WILKERSON, RUTH
    A WILKENS, FRANK B WILKES, BARRY C WILKIE, JANE D   20.____

21. HUGHES, MARY
    A HUGHES, MANUEL B HUGHES, MARGARET C HUGHES, MARTHA D   21.____

22. GODWIN, JAMES
    A GODFREY, SONDRA B GODMAN, GABRIEL C GODREAU, ROBERT D   22.____

23. NACHMAN, DAVID
    A NACHT, JAMES B NACK, SAUL C NACKENSON, LORI D   23.____

24. CASPER, LAURENCE
    A CASPER, LEONARD B CASPER, LESTER C CASPER, LINDA D   24.____

25. CULEN, ELLEN
    A CULHANE, JOHN B CULICHI, RADU C CULIN, TERRY D   25.____

KEY (CORRECT ANSWERS)

1. C
2. B
3. A
4. C
5. C

6. A
7. B
8. C
9. D
10. B

11. D
12. A
13. A
14. C
15. C

16. C
17. C
18. C
19. A
20. B

21. D
22. D
23. A
24. A
25. A

TEST 2

DIRECTIONS: For each of the following, you are given a name above and three other names in alphabetical order below. The letters A, B, C, and D stand for spaces where you could file the name. Find the CORRECT space for the name given above so that it will be in alphabetical order with the names below it. The letter that stands for that space is the answer to the question.

1. HARMAN, HENRY
   A HARLEY, LILLIAN B HARMER, RALPH C HARMON, CECIL D

   1.____

2. MANNING, JOHNSON
   A MANNING, JAMES B MANNING, JEROME C MANNING, JOHN D

   2.____

3. NOGUCHI, JANICE
   A NOEL, WALTER B NOGUET, DANIELLE C NOH, DAVID D

   3.____

4. PARRON, ALFONSE
   A PARRIS, LEON B PARRISH, LINDA C PARROTT, BETTY D

   4.____

5. GROSS, ELANA
   A GROSS, ELAINE B GROSS, ELIZABETH C GROSS, ELLIOT D

   5.____

6. HORSTMANN, ANNA
   A HORSMAN, ALLAN B HORST, VALERIE C HORSTMAN, JAMES D

   6.____

7. JONES, EMILY
   A JONES, ELMA B JONES, ELOISE C JONES, EMMA D

   7.____

8. LESSING, FRED
   A LESSER, MARTHA B LESSIN, ELLIE C LESSNER, ERWIN D

   8.____

9. ROSENBLUM, JULIUS
   A ROSENBLUTH, SYLVIA B ROSENBORG, ERIC C ROSENBURG, JANE D

   9.____

10. YOUNG, THEODORE
    A YOUNG, TERRY B YOUNG, THELMA C YOUNG, THOMAS D

    10.____

11. RENICK, KAREN
    A RENIE, JOSEPH B RENITA, JOSE C RENKO, DORIS D

    11.____

12. ADLER, HELEN
    A ADLER, HAROLD B ADLER, HARRY C ADLER, HENRY D

    12.____

13. BURKHARDT, ANN
    A BURKET, HARRIET B BURKHOLDER, CARL C BURKHOLZ, SCOTT D

    13.____

14. DE LUCA, PAUL
    A DE LUCA, JOHN B DE LUCIA, AUDREY C DE LUCIA, ROBERT D

    14.____

15. DEMBSKI, STEPHEN
    A DEMBLING, JOAN B DEMBNER, PETER C DEMBROW, HELEN D

    15.____

16. FLYNN, ARCHIE   16._____
    A FLYNN, AGNES B FLYNN, ANDREW C FLYNN, ANNMARIE D

17. GRAFFY, PAUL   17._____
    A GRAFMAN, ANDREW B GRAFSTEIN, BETTY C GRAFTON, MELVIN D

18. KERMIT, FRANK   18._____
    A KERMAN, LINDA B KERMISH, RHODA C KERMOYAN, MICKI D

19. METZLER, MAURICE   19._____
    A METZGER, ALFRED B METZIER, SONIA C METZINGER, PAUL D

20. PADDINGTON, TIMOTHY   20._____
    A PADDEN, MICHAEL B PADDISON, BRUCE C PADELL, EUNICE D

21. RICHARDSON, BLANCHE   21._____
    A RICHARDSON, BETTY B RICHARDSON, BEVERLY C RICHARDSON, BRENDA D

22. ISEKI, EMILE   22._____
    A ISELIN, CAROL B ISEN, RICHARD C ISENEE, CYNTHIA D

23. CONNELL, EUGENE   23._____
    A CONNELL, EDWARD B CONNELL, HELEN C CONNELL, HUGH D

24. MAC LEOD, LAURIE   24._____
    A MAC LEOD, LORNA B MC LANE, PAUL C MC LAREN, DUNCAN D

25. BOLE, KENNETH   25._____
    A BOLDEN, ROSIE B BOLDT, LINDA C BOLELLA, DENNIS D

KEY (CORRECT ANSWERS)

1.	B	11.	A
2.	D	12.	C
3.	B	13.	B
4.	C	14.	B
5.	B	15.	D
6.	D	16.	D
7.	C	17.	A
8.	C	18.	C
9.	A	19.	D
10.	C	20.	B

21. C
22. A
23. B
24. A
25. C

TEST 3

DIRECTIONS: For each of the following, you are given a name above and three other names in alphabetical order below. The letters A, B, C, and D stand for spaces where you could file the name. Find the CORRECT space for the name given above so that it will be in alphabetical order with the names below it. The letter that stands for that space is the answer to the question.

1. CARLISLE, ALAN
   A CARLINSKY, LEONA B CARLITOS, JUAN C CARLL, CHARLES D

2. COLLINS, KAREN
   A COLLINS, KATHLEEN B COLLINS, KATHRYN C COLLINS, KAY D

3. GALLOTTI, OSCAR
   A GALLONTY, FRANCIS B GALLOP, LILLIAN C GALLOU, ALEXIS D

4. MAHADY, JOHN
   A MAHADEO, PRATAB B MAHAJAN, ASHA C MAHARAJAH, MIARIAM D

5. WINGATE, REBECCA
   A WINGARD, LUCILLE B WINGAT, ROBERT C WINGER, HOLLY D

6. ZWEIGHAFT, FREDA
   A ZWEIG, BERTRAM B ZWEIGBAUM, BENJAMIN C ZWEIGENTHAL, DOROTHY D

7. MAXWELL, GEORGE
   A MAXWELL, EDWARD B MAXWELL, FRANK C MAXWELL, HARRIS D

8. O'DOHERTY, SALLY
   A ODETTE, CHARLES B ODIOTTI, MASSIE C ODNORALOV, MIKHAEL D

9. JAMES, ROGER
   A JAMIESON, KELLY B JAMNER, ELIZABETH C JAMPOLSKY, MILTON D

10. PADIN, FRANCIS
    A PADILLA, ANGELA B PADINGER, JENNY C PADLEY, RAYMOND D

11. AAARMAN, ALEC
    A AABY, JANE B AACH, ALBERT C AACHEN, HENRY D

12. BILLHARDT, PHILIP
    A BILLERA, FRANKLIN B BILLIG, LESLIE C BILLINGS, CAROL D

13. LADEROS, ELANA
    A LADENHEIM, HELENE B LADERMAN, SAM C LADHA, SANDRA D

14. PUCKERING, DENNIS
    A PUCKETT, AUDREY B PUCKNAT, JOHN C PUCKO, BENNY D

15. SCHOLZE, GEORGE
    A SCHOLNICK, LEONARD B SCHOLOSS, JACK C SCHOLZ, PAUL D

16. WILSON, MERYL
    A WILSON, MERIMAN B WILSON, MERRY C WILSON, MERRYL D
    16.____

17. ZUKOWSKI, MICHAEL
    A ZWACK, ALEXA B ZYKO, KATHERINE C ZYMAN, HERBERT D
    17.____

18. MC CANNA, THOMAS
    A MC CANN, GERALD B MC CANNA, JANET C MC CANTS, MOLLIE D
    18.____

19. PHILIPP, SUSANE
    A PHILIP, PETER B PHILIPOSE, ANDREW C PHILIPPE, BEATRICE D
    19.____

20. KINGPIN, PAUL
    A KINGDON, KENNETH B KINGMAN, JEAN C KINGOLD, RICHARD D
    20.____

21. HAMILTON, DONALD
    A HAMILTON, DON B HAMILTON, DOROTHY C HAMILTON, DOUGLAS D
    21.____

22. BAEL, ELAINE
    A BAELE, GUSTAVE B BAEN, JAMES C BAENA, ARIEL D
    22.____

23. BILL, KASEY
    A BILGINER, NATHAN B BILKAY, WILLIAM C BILLES, BRADFORD D
    23.____

24. CARLEN, ELLIOT
    A CARINO, NAN B CARLE, JOHN C CARLESI, ANTHONY D
    24.____

25. LOURIE, DONALD
    A LOUIE, ROSE B LOUIS, STEVE C LOVE, MARCIA D
    25.____

KEY (CORRECT ANSWERS)

1.	B	11.	A
2.	A	12.	B
3.	C	13.	C
4.	B	14.	A
5.	C	15.	D
6.	D	16.	D
7.	C	17.	A
8.	D	18.	C
9.	A	19.	C
10.	B	20.	D

21. B
22. A
23. C
24. C
25. C

TEST 4

DIRECTIONS: For each of the following, you are given a name above and three other names in alphabetical order below. The letters A, B, C, and D stand for spaces where you could file the name. Find the CORRECT space for the name given above so that it will be in alphabetical order with the names below it. The letter that stands for that space is the answer to the question.

1. DEMOPOULOS, GUS
   A DEMOPOULOS, DIMITRI B DEMOPOULOS, HELEN C DEMOPOULOS, LAURA D

   1.____

2. DRUMWRIGHT, BRUCE
   A DRUMMOND, RANDY B DRUMMUND, WALTER C DRUMRIGHT, JULIUS D

   2.____

3. GRAHAM, LETICIA
   A GRAHAM, LEON B GRAHAM, LEROY C GRAHAM, LESLIE D

   3.____

4. KELLEHER, KEVIN
   A KELLARD, WILLIAM B KELLEDY, JAMES C KELLEHER, KRISTINE D

   4.____

5. LIANG, JAN
   A LIANG, JIE B LIANG, JIN CHANG C LIANG, JIN HE D

   5.____

6. MOLINELLI, STEVE
   A MOLINAR, RICARDO B MOLINER, LOUISA C MOLINI, OSCAR D

   6.____

7. PARRILLA, EMANUEL
   A PARRAS, TONY B PARRETTA, JOSEPHINE C PARRETTA, NANCY D

   7.____

8. SILBERFARD, MILDRED
   A SILBERBERG, SEYMOUR B SILBERBLATT, JOHN C SILBERFARB, SYLVIA D

   8.____

9. TOLANI, ROHET
   A TOLAN, DOROTHY B TOLASSI, JOANNA C TOLBERT, ALICE D

   9.____

10. VIERA, DIANE
    A VIERA, DIANA B VIERA, ELLIOT C VIERA, JAMES D

    10.____

11. KLAUER, MICHAEL
    A KLAUBER, ALFRED B KLAUBERG, SUSAN C KLAUS, MARJORIE D

    11.____

12. REEVES, MARIE
    A REEVES, MATTHEW B REEVES, MELVIN C REEVES, ORALEE D

    12.____

13. DEL VALLE, JULIA
    A DEL VALLE, EMMA B DEL VALLE, GLORIA C DEL VALLE, JOSEPH D

    13.____

14. LAIO, SHU-YU
    A LAING, VINCENT B LAIRO, SCOTT C LAIS, STEVE D

    14.____

15. MENDEZ, ROBERTO
    A MENDELSON, SOL B MENDES, MAE C MENDOZA, HUGO D

    15.____

16. ALBRIGHT, LEE 16._____
    A ALBRACHT, MARIE B ALBRECHT, VICTOR C ALBRINK, JOAN D

17. CAIN, STEPHEN 17._____
    A CAIN, SAMUEL B CAIN, SHARON C CAIN, SIBOL D

18. HOPKOWITZ, THOMAS 18._____
    A HOPKINS, CYNTHIA B HOPPENFELD, DENIS C HOPPER, ELSA D

19. LUMBLY, KAREN 19._____
    A LUMBI, JENNY B LUME, JIMMIE C LUMEN, GAIL D

20. MAYER, MORTON 20._____
    A MAYER, MONROE B MAYER, MORRIS C MAYER, MYRON D

21. YOUNGER, LORRAINE 21._____
    A YOUNGHEM, THEODORE B YOUNGMAN, LEIF C YOUNGS, FRED D

22. THORSEN, HILDA 22._____
    A THORNWELL, PERCY B THORON, LLOYD C THORP, JACQUELINE D

23. MC DERMOTT, BETTY 23._____
    A MC DEARMON, WILLIAM B MC DEVITT, BERYL C MC DONAGH, DANIEL D

24. BLUMENTHAL, SIMON 24._____
    A BLUMENTHAL, SHIRLEY B BLUMENTHAL, SIDNEY C BLUMENTHAL, SOLOMON D

25. ERVINS, RICHARD 25._____
    A ERVIN, BERTHA B ERVING, THELMA C ERWIN, EUGENE D

KEY (CORRECT ANSWERS)

1. B
2. D
3. D
4. C
5. A

6. B
7. D
8. D
9. B
10. B

11. C
12. A
13. D
14. B
15. C

16. C
17. D
18. B
19. B
20. C

21. A
22. D
23. B
24. C
25. C

TEST 5

DIRECTIONS: For each of the following, you are given a name above and three other names in alphabetical order below. The letters A, B, C, and D stand for spaces where you could file the name. Find the CORRECT space for the name given above so that it will be in alphabetical order with the names below it. The letter that stands for that space is the answer to the question.

1. GUIDRY, THELMA
   A GUIDONE, GEORGE B GUIGLI, PAMELA C GUIGNON, DANIEL D

   1.____

2. JAMES, ALLAN
   A JAMES, ALMA B JAMES, AMY C JAMES, ANNA D

   2.____

3. LESSOFF, CONNIE
   A LESSIK, JAKE B LESSING, LEONARD C LESSNER, ADELE D

   3.____

4. MONTNER, LUIS
   A MONTEFIORE, ANDREW B MONTILLA, IRIS C MONTINI, ALEXANDRA D

   4.____

5. PHELPS, KENNETH
   A PHELEN, JAMES B PHELON, RANDY C PHETT, GARY D

   5.____

6. STAVSKY, STANLEY
   A STAVROS, MIKE B STAWSKI, LILLIAN C STAWSKI, NAOMI D

   6.____

7. GROSSMAN, WILL
   A GROSSMAN, WENDY B GROSSMANN, WAYNE C GROSSMANN, WILLA D

   7.____

8. IRES, JEFFREY
   A IRENA, THOMAS B IRENE, JAY C IRES, HOWARD D

   8.____

9. NIKOLAOU, CHRISTINE
   A NIKOLAIS, GERRARD B NIKOLAKAKOS, GEORGE C NIKOLATOS, HARRY D

   9.____

10. TURCO, KEITH
    A TURCHIN, DEBORAH B TURCI, GINA C TURCK, KATHRYN D

    10.____

11. WORLEY, DIANE
    A WORMAN, STELLA B WORMER, SARA C WORMLEY, ROBERT D

    11.____

12. DRUSIN, GUY
    A DRURY, JESSICA B DRUSE, KEN C DRUSS, THERESA D

    12.____

13. LYONS, JAMES
    A LYONS, ERNST B LYONS, INGRID C LYONS, KEVIN D

    13.____

14. NOBLE, BERNARD
    A NOBEL, LOUISE B NOBILE, DENNIS C NOBIS, JAMES D

    14.____

15. O'DELL, ERIN
    A O'DAY, PATRICIA B O'DEA, MAUREEN C O'DELL, GWYNN D

    15.____

16. POUPON, LOUIS
    A POULSON, SIMON B POURE, DAMIAN C POURIDAS, CARMEN D

16. ____

17. REMEY, NAOMI
    A REMES, STUART B REMEZ, ALFREDO C REMIEN, ROBERT D

17. ____

18. WATSON, LAURENCE
    A WATSON, LENORA B WATSON, LEONARD C WATSON, LLOYD D

18. ____

19. AMSILI, MORTON
    A AMSDEN, ESTHER B AMSEL, HYMAN C ARES, MEYER D

19. ____

20. CLEMMONS, BERTHA
    A CLEMENT, GILBERT B CLEMINSON, DEAN C CLEMONS, GLADYS D

20. ____

21. LAMPERT, EDNA
    A LAMPIER, JANICE B LAMPKIN, ALYCE C LAMPKOWSKI, DENNIS D

21. ____

22. LIBERTO, DON
    A LIBERMAN, MATTIE B LIBERSON, MIRIAM C LIBERTY, ARTHUR D

22. ____

23. REVENZON, ISABELLA
    A REVELEY, RUTH B REVELLE, GRACE C REVERE, EDITH D

23. ____

24. BURKHALTER, HAZEL
    A BURKE, WINSTON B BURKETT, BENJAMIN C BURKEY, WAYNE D

24. ____

25. DORSEY, HAROLD
    A DOSHER, EILEEN B DOSHIRE, BURTON C DOSSIL, RICHARD D

25. ____

KEY (CORRECT ANSWERS)

1.	B	11.	A
2.	A	12.	C
3.	D	13.	C
4.	D	14.	D
5.	C	15.	C
6.	B	16.	B
7.	B	17.	B
8.	D	18.	A
9.	C	19.	C
10.	D	20.	C

21. A
22. C
23. C
24. D
25. A

TEST 6

DIRECTIONS: For each of the following, you are given a name above and three other names in alphabetical order below. The letters A, B, C, and D stand for spaces where you could file the name. Find the CORRECT space for the name given above so that it will be in alphabetical order with the names below it. The letter that stands for that space is the answer to the question.

1. HATFIELD, NICOLA
   A HATCHER, JOHN B HATELY, BRIAN C HATGIS, ELLEN D

   1.____

2. IVANOFF, HELENA
   A IVAN, LEONARD B IVANOV, SERGE C IVANY, EMERY D

   2.____

3. KELKER, NORMAN
   A KELFER, STEPHANE B KELING, JAY C KELISON, ABE D

   3.____

4. ROGGENBURG, LEE
   A ROGERS, SHARON B ROGET, ALLAN C ROGGERO, MORGAN D

   4.____

5. SMITH, ALENA
   A SMITH, AARON B SMITH, AGNES C SMITH, ALBERT D

   5.____

6. ZOLOR, RONALD
   A ZOLNAK, SUSANNA B ZOLOTH, SAMUEL C ZOLOTO, PEARL D

   6.____

7. ERRICH, GRETCHEN
   A ERREICH, RENE B ERRERA, STEVEN C ERRETT, ALICE D

   7.____

8. CARDWELL, MELASAN
   A CARDUCCI, RONALD B CARDULLO, MIKE C CARDY, FREDRIK D

   8.____

9. MOFFAT, SARAH
   A MOFFET, JONATHAN B MOFFIE, LISA C MOFFITT, LAUREN D

   9.____

10. PARRINO, WAYNE
    A PARRETTA, MICHELE B PARRILLA, BERNIE C PARRINELLO, CARRIE D

    10.____

11. PINSLEY, SETH
    A PINSKY, GLORIA B PINSON, BENNET C PINTADO, MARIE D

    11.____

12. FREEMAN, ELMIRA
    A FREEMAN, EDITH B FREEMAN, ERIC C FREEMAN, ETHEL D

    12.____

13. BERLINGER, SOPHIE
    A BERLEY, DAVID B BERLIND, ARNOLD C BERLINGER, FREDA D

    13.____

14. ANIELLO, JOSEPH
    A ANGULO, ADOLFO B ANHALT, LINDA C ANIBAL, VINCENT D

    14.____

15. LACHER, LEO
    A LACHET, MARGARET B LACHINI, KAY C LACHIVER, ANDREA D

    15.____

16. ROBINSON, MARION
    A ROBINSON, MARCIA B ROBINSON, MARGARET C ROBINSON, MARIETTA D
    16.___

17. ULRICH, DENNIS
    A ULMAN, CANDY B ULMER, TED C ULRIED, RICHARD D
    17.___

18. ASHINSKY, ROSS
    A ASHKAR, MICHAEL B ASHKE, PAUL C ASHKIN, ROBERTA D
    18.___

19. LITVAK, DARRELL
    A LITUCHY, BEVERLY B LITVIN, SAM C LITWACK, MARTIN D
    19.___

20. SLATTERY, GERALD
    A SLATER, NELLIE B SLATKIN, HEIDI C SLATKY, IRVING D
    20.___

21. MCCANTS, GEORGIA
    A MCCANN, CHERYL B MCCANNA, THOMAS C MCCARDELL, GARY D
    21.___

22. HARMER, AVA
    A HARLOW, JULES B HARLSON, NORMAN C HARMEL, SHARON D
    22.___

23. CALDERONE, PHILIP
    A CALDERIN, ANA B CALDON, WALTER C CALDRON, MICHELE D
    23.___

24. GINSBURG, ISAAC
    A GINSBURG, EDWARD B GINSBURG, GERALD C GINSBURG, HILDA D
    24.___

25. LEE, LEIGH
    A LEE, LELA B LEE, LELAND C LEE, LEON D
    25.___

KEY (CORRECT ANSWERS)

1.	C		11.	B
2.	B		12.	B
3.	D		13.	D
4.	C		14.	D
5.	D		15.	A
6.	B		16.	D
7.	D		17.	C
8.	C		18.	A
9.	A		19.	B
10.	D		20.	D

21. C
22. D
23. B
24. D
25. A

TEST 7

DIRECTIONS: For each of the following, you are given a name above and three other names in alphabetical order below. The letters A, B, C, and D stand for spaces where you could file the name. Find the CORRECT space for the name given above so that it will be in alphabetical order with the names below it. The letter that stands for that space is the answer to the question.

1. POWERS, PHYLLIS
A POWELL, HATTIE B POWER, EDWARD C POWLETT, WENDY D

1.____

2. SILVERA, IRWIN
A SILVA, ANGEL B SILVANO, FRANK C SILVERIA, ANNA D

2.____

3. BACHRACH, DAN
A BACHMANN, DONNA B BACHNER, LESTER C BACHOWSKI, JEWEL D

3.____

4. RIVERA, RAMON
A RIVAS, ERICA B RIVES, SHARON C RIVIER, CLAUDE D

4.____

5. WEINSTOCK, JEFFREY
A WEINSTEIN, PAUL B WEINSTONE, ALAN C WEINTRAUB, MARCI D

5.____

6. AMANDA, STEPHAN
A AMADO, DANIELLO B AMALIA, JOSE C AMAR, LISA D

6.____

7. HERRON, LOUIS
A HERSCH, JACK B HERSCHELL, GREGORY C HERSCHER, GAIL D

7.____

8. REEDY, ARTHUR
A REED, ALEX B REESE, JOHN C REEVE, DAVE D

8.____

9. FLORIN, RAYMOND
A FLORENTINO, PAULA B FLORES, MITCHEL C FLORIAN, CARLO D

9.____

10. HOROWITZ, ELLIOT
A HOROWITZ, FRANKLIN B HOROWITZ, IRA C HOROWITZ, JOAN D

10.____

11. KNOPFLER, WOODY
A KNOBLER, HENRY B KNOLL, GEORGE C KNOPF, LAURA D

11.____

12. OTIN, JENNIFER
A OTERO, ALBERT B OTHON, DOROTHY C OTIS, JAMES D

12.____

13. SACHA, IRENE
A SACCO, HEATHER B SACHNER, JULIE C SACHS, DAVID D

13.____

14. WORTHY, PRISCILLA
A WORTH, ROBERT B WORTHINGTON, SUSAN C WORTMAN, MYRA D

14.____

15. ZUCKERMAN, GARY
A ZUKER, JEROME B ZUKOWSKI, CHRIS C ZULACK, JOHN D

15.____

2 (#7)

16. BRIEGER, CLARENCE
    A BRIEF, SIGMUND B BRIELLE, JEAN C BRIELOFF, SAUL D   16.____

17. FOSTER, AGNES
    A FOSTER, ADDIE B FOSTER, ALBERT C FOSTER, ALICE D   17.____

18. LIBERSTEIN, MIRIAM
    A LIBERMAN, HERMAN B LIBERSON, RUBIN C LIBERT, NAT D   18.____

19. PRICKETT, DELORES
    A PRICE, WILLIAM B PRICHARD, STEPHANY C PRITCHETT, KENNETH D   19.____

20. TRIBBLE, RITA
    A TRIAS, JOSE B TRIBBIT, CHARLES C TRIBE, SIENNA D   20.____

21. ZOBEL, MAX
    A ZOBACK, DERRICK B ZOBALI, KIERSTAN C ZOBERG, STUART D   21.____

22. HOTRA, WALTER
    A HOTT, NELL B HOTTENSEN, ROBERT C HOTTON, BRUCE D   22.____

23. MICHELL, CARL
    A MICHELE, KAREN B MICHELMAN, BERTHA C MICHELS, GLORIA D   23.____

24. RAFFERTY, GEORGE
    A RAFFERTY, HAROLD B RAFFERTY, KEVIN C RAFFERTY, LUCILLE D   24.____

25. OLIVIERI, ALLAN
    A OLIVIERO, FRANK B OLIVRY, RAUL C OLIZEIRA, CHARLES D   25.____

KEY (CORRECT ANSWERS)

1. C
2. C
3. D
4. B
5. B

6. C
7. A
8. B
9. D
10. A

11. D
12. C
13. B
14. C
15. A

16. B
17. B
18. C
19. C
20. C

21. C
22. A
23. B
24. A
25. A

NAME AND NUMBER COMPARISONS

COMMENTARY

This test seeks to measure your ability and disposition to do a job carefully and accurately, your attention to exactness and preciseness of detail, your alertness and versatility in discerning similarities and differences between things, and your power in systematically handling written language symbols.

It is actually a test of your ability to do academic and/or clerical work, using the basic elements of verbal (qualitative) and mathematical (quantitative) learning—words <u>and</u> numbers.

EXAMINATION SECTION

TEST 1

DIRECTIONS: Questions 1 through 6 consist of sets of names and addresses. In each question, the name and address in Column II should be an exact copy of the name and address in Column II. *PRINT IN THE SPACE AT THE RIGHT THE LETTER*
    A. if there is a mistake only in the name
    B. if there is a mistake only in the address
    C. if there is a mistake in both name and address
    D. If there is no mistake in either name or address

SAMPLE:
Michael Filbert	Michael Filbert
456 Reade Street	644 Reade Street
New York, N.Y. 10013	New York, N.Y. 10013

Since there is a mistake only in the address, the answer is B.

1.   Esta Wong   Esta Wang   1.____
    141 West 68 St.   141 West 68 St.
    New York, N.Y. 10023   New York, N.Y. 10023

2.   Dr. Alberto Grosso   Dr. Alberto Grosso   2.____
    3475 12th Avenue   3475 12th Avenue
    Brooklyn, N.Y. 11218   Brooklyn, N.Y. 11218

3.   Mrs. Ruth Bortlas   Ms. Ruth Bortias   3.____
    482 Theresa Ct.   482 Theresa Ct.
    Far Rockaway, N.Y. 11691   Far Rockaway, N.Y. 11169

4.   Mr. and Mrs. Howard Fox   Mr. and Mrs. Howard Fox   4.____
    2301 Sedgwick Ave.   231 Sedgwick Ave.
    Bronx, N.Y. 10468   Bronx, N.Y. 10468

5.   Miss Marjorie Black   Miss Margorie Black   5.____
    223 East 23 Street   223 East 23 Street
    New York, N.Y. 10010   New York, N.Y. 10010

2 (#1)

6. Michelle Herman　　　　　Michelle Hermann　　　　　　　　　　　　6.____
   806 Valley Rd.　　　　　　806 Valley Dr.
   Old Tappan, N.J. 07675　　Old Tappan, N.J. 07675

KEY (CORRECT ANSWERS)

1. A
2. D
3. C
4. B
5. A
6. C

TEST 2

DIRECTIONS: Questions 1 through 6 consist of sets of names and addresses. In each question, the name and address in Column II should be an exact copy of the name and address in Column II. *PRINT IN THE SPACE AT THE RIGHT THE LETTER*

    A. if there is a mistake only in the name
    B. if there is a mistake only in the address
    C. if there is a mistake in both name and address
    D. If there is no mistake in either name or address

1. Ms. Joan Kelly
313 Franklin Ave.
Brooklyn, N.Y. 11202

   Ms. Joan Kielly
318 Franklin Ave.
Brooklyn, N.Y. 11202

1.____

2. Mrs. Eileen Engel
47-24 86 Road
Queens, N.Y. 11122

   Mrs. Ellen Engel
47-24 86 Road
Queens, N.Y. 11122

2.____

3. Marcia Michaels
213 E. 81 St.
New York, N.Y. 10012

   Marcia Michaels
213 E. 81 St.
New York, N.Y. 10012

3.____

4. Rev. Edward J. Smyth
1401 Brandeis Street
San Francisco, Calif. 96201

   Rev. Edward J. Smyth
1401 Brandies Street
San Francisco, Calif. 96201

4.____

5. Alicia Rodriguez
24-68 81 St.
Elmhurst, N.Y. 11122

   Alicia Rodriquez
2468 81 St.
Elmhurst, N.Y. 11122

5.____

6. Ernest Eissemann
21 Columbia St.
New York, N.Y. 10007

   Ernest Eisermann
21 Columbia St.
New York, N.Y. 10007

6.____

KEY (CORRECT ANSWERS)

1. C
2. A
3. D
4. B
5. C
6. A

TEST 3

DIRECTIONS: Questions 1 through 8 consist of names, locations, and telephone numbers. In each question, the name, location and number in Column II should be an exact copy of the name, location, and number in Column I. *PRINT IN THE SPACE AT THE RIGHT THE LETTER*
- A. if there is a mistake in one line only
- B. if there is a mistake in two lines only
- C. if there is a mistake in three lines only
- D. if there are no mistakes in any of the lines

1. Ruth Lang　　　　　　　　　　　　　Ruth Lang　　　　　　　　　　　　1._____
   EAM Bldg., Room C101　　　　　　　EAM Bldg., Room C110
   625-2000, ext. 765　　　　　　　　　625-2000, ext. 765

2. Anne Marie Ionozzi　　　　　　　　Anna Marie Ionozzi　　　　　　　　2._____
   Investigations, Room 827　　　　　Investigation, Room 827
   576-4000, ext. 832　　　　　　　　　566-4000, ext. 832

3. Willard Jameson　　　　　　　　　Willard Jamieson　　　　　　　　　3._____
   Fm C Bldg. Room 687　　　　　　　Fm C Bldg. Room 687
   454-3010　　　　　　　　　　　　　454-3010

4. Joanne Zimmermann　　　　　　　Joanne Zimmermann　　　　　　　　4._____
   Bldg. SW, Room 314　　　　　　　　Bldg. SW, Room 314
   532-4601　　　　　　　　　　　　　532-4601

5. Carlyle Whetstone　　　　　　　　Caryle Whetstone　　　　　　　　　5._____
   Payroll Division-A, Room 212A　　Payroll Division-A, Room 212A
   262-5000, ext. 471　　　　　　　　262-5000, ext. 417

6. Kenneth Chiang　　　　　　　　　Kenneth Chiang　　　　　　　　　　6._____
   Legal Council, Room 9745　　　　 Legal Counsel, Room 9745
   (201) 416-9100, ext. 17　　　　　 (201) 416-9100, ext. 17

7. Ethel Koenig　　　　　　　　　　 Ethel Hoenig　　　　　　　　　　　7._____
   Personnel Services Div, Rm 433　 Personal Services Div, Rm 433
   635-7572　　　　　　　　　　　　　635-7527

8. Joyce Ehrhardt　　　　　　　　　 Joyce Ehrhart　　　　　　　　　　 8._____
   Office of Administrator, Rm W56　Office of Administrator, Rm W56
   387-8706　　　　　　　　　　　　　387-7806

KEY (CORRECT ANSWERS)

1. A
2. C
3. A
4. D
5. B
6. A
7. C
8. B

TEST 4

DIRECTIONS: Each of Questions 1 through 10 gives the identification number and name of a person who has received treatment at a certain hospital. You are to choose the option (A, B, C, or D) which has EXACTLY the same number and name as those given in the question.

SAMPLE QUESTION:
123765 Frank Y. Jones
- A. 123675 Frank Y. Jones
- B. 123765 Frank T. Jones
- C. 123765 Frank Y. Jones
- D. 123765 Frank Y. Jones

The correct answer is D, because it is the only option showing the identification number and name exactly as they are in the sample question.

1. 754898 Diane Malloy
   - A. 745898 Diane Malloy
   - B. 754898 Dion Malloy
   - C. 754898 Diane Malloy
   - D. 754898 Diane Maloy

1.____

2. 661818 Ferdinand Figueroa
   - A. 661818 Ferdinand Figeuroa
   - B. 661618 Ferdinand Figueroa
   - C. 661818 Ferdnand Figueroa
   - D. 661818 Ferdinand Figueroa

2.____

3. 100101 Norman D. Braustein
   - A. 100101 Norman D. Braustein
   - B. 101001 Norman D. Braustein
   - C. 100101 Norman P. Braustien
   - D. 100101 Norman D. Bruastein

3.____

4. 838696 Robert Kittredge
   - A. 838969 Robert Kittredge
   - B. 838696 Robert Kittredge
   - C. 388696 Robert Kittredge
   - D. 838696 Robert Kittridge

4.____

5. 243716 Abraham Soletsky
   - A. 243716 Abrahm Soletsky
   - B. 243716 Abraham Solestky
   - C. 243176 Abraham Soletsky
   - D. 243716 Abraham Soletsky

5.____

6. 981121 Phillip M. Maas
   - A. 981121 Phillip M. Mass
   - B. 981211 Phillip M. Maas
   - C. 981121 Phillip M. Maas
   - D. 981121 Phillip N. Maas

6.____

7. 786556 George Macalusso
   - A. 785656 George Macalusso
   - B. 786556 George Macalusso
   - C. 786556 George Maculusso
   - D. 786556 George Macluasso

7.____

8. 639472 Eugene Weber
   - A. 639472 Eugene Weber
   - B. 639472 Eugene Webre
   - C. 693472 Eugene Weber
   - D. 639742 Eugene Weber

8.____

2 (#4)

9. 724936 John J. Lomonaco					9._____
   A. 724936 John J. Lomanoco		B. 724396 John L. Lomonaco
   C. 7224936 John J. Lomonaco		D. 724936 John J. Lamonaco

10. 899868 Michael Schnitzer					10._____
    A. 899868 Micheal Schnitzer		B. 898968 Michael Schnizter
    C. 899688 Michael Schnitzer		D. 899868 Michael Schnitzer

KEY (CORRECT ANSWERS)

1. C   6. C
2. D   7. B
3. A   8. A
4. B   9. C
5. D   10. D

NAME AND NUMBER CHECKING
EXAMINATION SECTION
TEST 1

DIRECTIONS: Each question consists of a name, address, and social security number, arranged in 2 lists. List I is correct, but some mistakes were made in copying the information to List II. For each question, you must check to see if there are any mistakes in List II. Mark your answer A if there are no mistakes in List II. Mark your answer B if there is a mistake in List II.

<u>LIST I</u>   <u>LIST II</u>

1. BRUCE CHAMBERS
   211 MIAMI ROAD
   879-86-3417

   Bruce Chambers
   211 Miami Blvd.
   879-86-3417

   1.____

2. PAUL NEADERLANDER
   2 CIRCLE DRIVE
   294-04-7199

   Paul Neaderlander
   2 Circle Drive
   294-04-7199

   2.____

3. ERNESTINE THOMPSON
   87 WEST 9TH STREET
   949-09-7211

   Ernestine Thompson
   87 West 9th Street
   949-09-7211

   3.____

4. JOANNE MYERS
   16 TOPPLETREE ROAD
   655-29-0733

   Joanne Meyers
   16 Toppletree Road
   655-29-0733

   4.____

5. EMILY JONES
   40 HADLEY AVENUE
   269-79-0011

   Emily Jones
   40 Hadley Avenue
   269-09-0011

   5.____

6. FRANKLIN GRETSKY
   99 DOLPHIN AVENUE
   879-09-2111

   Franklin Geretsky
   99 Dolphin Avenue
   879-09-2111

   6.____

7. BARBERA EVANS
   16 BARNABY LANE
   269-04-7711

   Barbara Evans
   16 Barnaby Lane
   269-04-7711

   7.____

8. RICHARD BELTZER
   119 MONTAGUE STREET
   079-29-0473

   Richard Beltzer
   119 Montague Street
   079-29-0473

   8.____

9. LEE TEMPLE
   498 EAST16TH N.W.
   249-07-3711

   Lee Temple
   498 East 61st N.W.
   249-07-3711

   9.____

2 (#1)

LIST I	LIST II	
10. MADELINE DOUGHERTY 330 TIMBERLANE ROAD 079-29-0473	Madeline Dougherty 119 Montague Street 079-29-0473	10.____
11. PETULIA FOX 16 MANN TERRACE 749-09-2911	Petulia Fox 16 Mann Terrace 749-09-0911	11.____
12. MARION ROLLINS 279 MANOR ROAD 478-86-2711	Marion Rollins 279 Manor Road 478-86-2711	12.____
13. ROBERTA JACKSON 2 PAINTERS LANE 876-27-9449	Roberta Jackson 2 Printers Lane 876-27-9449	13.____
14. LYNN PURCELL 1681 FORD ROAD 279-09-8733	Lynn Purcell 1681 Ford Road 279-09-8733	14.____
15. MANNY EISEN 27-11 OCEAN BLVD. 879-21-4711	Manny Eisen 27-11 Ocean Blvd. 879-21-4711	15.____
16. MARK HANOVER 47 TULIP LANE 279-08-0771	Mark Hanover 47 Tulip Lane 279-08-0771	16.____
17. MARIANNE MATTHEWS 81 RIVERSIDE DRIVE 871-29-4211	Marianne Matthews 81 Riverside Drive 871-29-4211	17.____
18. CHARLES DOUGLAS 27 MONTGMERY ROAD 879-29-4011	Charles Douglas 27 Montgomry Road 879-29-4011	18.____
19. LONNY DONALDSON 87 PETERS AVENUE 277-63-0739	Lonny Donaldson 87 Peters Avenue 277-63-9739	19.____
20. PATRICK MCCOLLOUGH 168 BARRON STREET 899-26-4733	Patrick McCollough 168 Barron Street 899-26-4733	20.____
21. JOHN ALEXANDER 425 WEST END AVENUE 876-01-2371	John Alexanders 425 West End Avenue 876-01-2371	21.____

3 (#1)

LIST I	LIST II	
22. PHILIP MANCHESTER 86 GIBBONS DRIVE 297-83-0124	Philip Manchester 86 Gibbons Drive 297-38-0124	22.____
23. ALYSSIA SARKOV 1086A ELM STREET 249-66-0371	Alyssia Sarkov 1086A Elm Street 249-66-0371	23.____
24. TREMONT KLEE 9272 YORKVILLE ROAD 265-54-2793	Tremont Klee 9272 Yorkville Road 244-78-0733	24.____
25. EVAN FISCH 824 BELLOWS LANE 244-78-0733	Evan Fisch 842 Bellows Lane 244-78-0733	25.____

KEY (CORRECT ANSWERS)

ERROR IN LIST II

1. B 211 Miami <u>Blvd.</u>
2. A
3. A
4. B M<u>e</u>yers
5. B 269-<u>0</u>9-0011

6. B G<u>e</u>retsky
7. B Barb<u>a</u>ra
8. A
9. B 498 East <u>61</u>st Street
10. A

11. B 749-09-<u>0</u>911
12. A
13. B 2 P<u>r</u>inters Lane
14. A
15. A

16. A
17. A
18. B 27 Montgo<u>mr</u>y Road
19. A
20. A

21. B Alexander<u>s</u>
22. B 297-<u>38</u>-0124
23. A
24. B 265-54-2<u>973</u>
25. B 8<u>4</u>2 Bellows Lane

TEST 2

DIRECTIONS: Each question consists of a name, address, and social security number, arranged in 2 lists. List I is correct, but some mistakes were made in copying the information to List II. For each question, you must check to see if there are any mistakes in List II. Mark your answer A if there are no mistakes in List II. Mark your answer B if there is a mistake in List II.

LIST I | LIST II

1. CONNIE SISKIN
4 ELIZABETH LANE
679-24-2211

Connie Siskin
4 Elizabeth Lane
679-24-2211

1.____

2. YOLANDA PRINCIPE
19 FORREST STREET
876-24-6711

Yolanda Principe
19 Forest Street
876-24-6711

2.____

3. MADELINE PHILLIPS
16 STONEY POINT ROAD
279-24-0779

Madeline Phillips
16 Stoney Point Road
279-24-0799

3.____

4. OSVALDO SOUZA
1681 YORK AVENUE
678-23-4271

Osvaldo Souza
1681 York Avenue
678-23-4271

4.____

5. CATHERINE ELLISON
4248th AVENUE S.W.
269-72-7388

Catharine Ellison
4248th Avenue S.W.
269-72-7388

5.____

6. FRANKLIN AQUINO
827 RYDERS LANE
777-01-2455

Franklin Aquino
827 Ryders Lane
777-01-2455

6.____

7. STEPHANIE FOREMAN
1096 FEDERAL CIRCLE
287-79-0334

Stepfanie Foreman
1096 Federal Circle
287-79-0334

7.____

8. MICHAEL O'NEILL
16 FLORENCE ROAD
989-76-7661

Michael O'Neil
16 Florence Road
989-76-7661

8.____

9. SANDRA MORRIS
16 BELMONT AVENUE
248-16-7111

Sandra Morris
16 Belmont Avenue
248-16-1711

9.____

10. FRANCIS MURRAY
2 TARKINGTON AVENUE
755-81-1211

Francis Murray
2 Tarkington Avenue
755-81-1211

10.____

2 (#2)

11. ADRIAN GOLDSTEIN
14 CIRCLE DRIVE NORTH
798-81-2171

Adrien Goldstein
14 Circle Drive North
798-81-2171

11.____

12. PHYLICIA FOXX
191 MYERS ROAD
678-01-2371

Phylicia Foxx
191 Myers Road
678-01-2371

12.____

13. MARION NORDSTROM
249 WEST 86TH STREET
279-49-0711

Marion Nordstrom
249 West 86th Street
248-79-0711

13.____

14. RONALD PLOTTSKIN
2 AMELIA AVENUE
544-36-0781

Ronald Plottkin
2 Amelia Avenue
544-36-0781

14.____

15. WILLIAM DWYER
21 MIDDLE STREET
876-81-8112

William Dwyer
21 Middle Street
876-18-8112

15.____

16. PETER FILMORE
788 PARK LANE
799-23-0142

Peter Filmore
788 Park Lane
788-23-0142

16.____

17. KAREN STANISLAVSKY
498 TERMINAL ACCESS ROAD
611-27-4111

Karen Stanislawsky
498 Terminal Access Road
611-27-4111

17.____

18. EDWARD PUSHKIN
67-89 MAPLE STREET
278-86-7899

Edward Pushkin
67-89 Maple Street
278-68-7899

18.____

19. CHRISTINA FABRIKANT
116 EAST 111TH STREET
249-09-7381

Christine Fabrikant
116 East 111th Street
249-09-7381

19.____

20. CHARLES KLEINMAN
1061 MADISON AVENUE
354-86-1102

Charles Kleinman
1061 Madison Avenue
354-86-1102

20.____

21. DOMINIC LACATA
33 GREENWICH AVENUE
274-86-0311

Dominic Lacata
33 Greenich Avenue
274-86-0311

21.____

22. PAUL LEVY
1086A 20TH STREET
102-80-0116

Paul Levy
1086A 20th Street
102-80-0116

22.____

3 (#2)

LIST I	LIST II	
23. PATRICIA MEADE 141 CABRINI BLVD. 689-37-2371	Patricia Meade 141 Cabrinni Blvd. 689-37-2371	23._____
24. MORRIS FELINSKY 9 PRUDENCE PLACE 789-36-2499	Morris Felinsky 9 Prudence Place 789-63-2499	24._____
25. ESTER PRADO 17 EAST 16TH STREET 246-03-0919	Ester Prado 17 East 15th Street 246-03-0919	25._____
26. BARBARA POWELL 75 MONTGOMERY ROAD 879-23-6754	Barbara Powell 75 Montgomery Road 879-32-6754	26._____
27. RALPH BELLACCIO 269 WEST 76TH STREET 268-89-9442	Ralph Bellaccio 269-West 76th Street 269-89-9442	27._____
28. DENISE DAVIS 100 MORNINGSIDE DRIVE 249-29-6602	Denise Davis 100 Morningside Drive 248-29-6602	28._____
29. ANGELA TORRES 48 CHRISTOPHER STREET 649-09-2366	Angela Torres 48 Christopher Street 649-09-2366	29._____
30. LOUISE CHAPMAN 16 HATFIELD ROAD 682-66-5432	Louise Chapman 16 Hatfield Road 682-66-5342	30._____

KEY (CORRECT ANSWERS)

		ERROR IN LIST II
1.	A	
2.	B	19 Fo<u>re</u>st Street
3.	B	279-34-07<u>9</u>9
4.	A	
5.	B	Cath<u>a</u>rine
6.	A	
7.	B	Step<u>f</u>anie
8.	B	O'Neil<u>_</u>
9.	B	248-16-<u>17</u>11
10.	A	
11.	B	
12.	A	
13.	B	2<u>4</u>9-79-0711
14.	B	Plot<u>t</u>kin
15.	B	876-<u>18</u>-8112
16.	B	7<u>8</u>9-23-0142
17.	B	Stanisla<u>w</u>sky
18.	B	278-<u>68</u>-7899
19.	B	Christin<u>e</u>
20.	A	
21.	B	33 Gree<u>n</u>ich Avenue
22.	A	
23.	B	Cabri<u>n</u>ni
24.	B	789-<u>63</u>-2499
25.	B	17 East 1<u>5</u>th Street
26.	B	879-<u>32</u>-6754
27.	B	26<u>9</u>-89-9442
28.	A	
29.	A	
30.	B	682-66-5<u>34</u>2

TEST 3

DIRECTIONS: Each question consists of a name, address, and social security number, arranged in 2 lists. List I is correct, but some mistakes were made in copying the information to List II. For each question, you must check to see if there are any mistakes in List II. Mark your answer A if there are no mistakes in List II. Mark your answer B if there is a mistake in List II.

LIST I

LIST II

1. HATTIE BERKER
109-49 EOTH STREET N.W.
268-38-4211

   Hattie Berker
   109-49 40th Street N.W.
   268-38-4211

   1.____

3. MANUEL FELICIAS
2938 CANADA BLVD.
168-33-9742

   Manuel Felicias
   2968 Canada Blvd.
   168-33-9742

   2.____

3. BURTON BALANOWSKI
76 HADLEY BLVD.
286-49-2311

   Burton Balanowski
   76 Hadley Blvd.
   286-49-3211

   3.____

4. DAVID CONKLIN
298 HOBOKEN STREET
168-28-3798

   David Conklin
   298 Hoboken Street
   168-28-3798

   4.____

5. MICHELLE ROGET
10 AGAWAM ROAD
279-39-3722

   Michele Roget
   10 Agawam Road
   279-39-3722

   5.____

6. HANNA GREENE
141 WEST 9TH STREET
876-36-3611

   Hanna Greene
   141 West 9th Street
   876-36-3611

   6.____

7. BARRY NEWMARK
42 TODD STREET
867-32-7399

   Barry Newmark
   42 Todd Street
   867-23-7399

   7.____

8. MELISSA FEUTREL
898 HERALD SQUARE
267-79-2388

   Melissa Feutrel
   898 Herald Square
   276-79-2388

   8.____

9. AMY KINGSLEY
428 TOWNSHIP LANE
771-17-2377

   Amy Kingsely
   428 Township Lane
   771-17-2377

   9.____

10. PAMELA WINCHESTER
1781 DELUTH AVENUE
876-18-2733

    Pamela Winchester
    178 DeLuth Avenue
    876-18-2733

    10.____

2 (#3)

LIST I	LIST II	
11. HORACE BUELOW 1683 YORK STREET S.W. 478-09-7332	Horace Buelow 1863 York Street S.W. 478-09-7332	11.____
12. ANNA MARIA BARDONNA 11 MAGENTA ROAD 679-23-0734	Anna Maria Bardonna 11 Margenta Road 679-23-0734	12.____
13. CECIL PAXTON 61 EAST 93RD STREET 679-03-4992	Cecil Paxton 61 East 93rd Street 678-03-4992	13.____
14. TAUREAN SIMPSON 1429-89 111TH STREET N.W. 479-83-7655	Taurean Simpson 1429-81 111TH Street N.W. 479-83-7655	14.____
15. KATHY KETCHUM 4711 GRANT STREET 879-23-3754	Kathy Ketchum 40711 Grand Street 879-23-3754	15.____
16. JANET SCHAEFFER 27 CALDWELL AVENUE 683-23-7249	Janet Schaffer 27 Caldwell Avenue 683-23-7249	16.____
17. JAMES COBALT 25 CENTER CITY PARK 223-83-4947	James Cobalt 25 Center City Park 223-83-4749	17.____
18. CONNIE KELINSKI 97 CONKLIN STREET 776-25-9631	Connie Kelinski 97 Conklin Street 776-25-9631	18.____
19. HENRY ROUSSEAU 2 SIENNA DRIVE 777-07-2300	Henry Rousseau 2 Sienna Drive 777-07-2399	19.____
20. PETER MARKHAM 421 RYAN ROAD 687-37-4381	Peter Markham 412 Ryan Road 687-37-4381	20.____
21. WILLIAM JAMES 4798 BOSTON HWY. 679-23-4755	William Janes 4798 Boston Hwy. 679-23-4755	21.____
22. EDWARD STRUTTHERS 1611-27 UNION STREET 722-29 4785	Edward Struthers 1611-29-4785 722-29-4785	22.____

3 (#3)

LIST I	LIST II	
23. HANNA ROSENBLATT 798 COMMERCE STREET 211-01-0733	Hanna Rosenblatt 798 Commerce Street 211-01-0733	23.____
24. BEVERLY KINGSLEY 23 LAMBERT ROAD 429-79-3337	Beverly Kingsley 23 Lambert Road 429-73-3337	24.____
25. TIMOTHY TEMPKIN 334 E. 93RD STREET 233-09-4555	Timothy Tempkin 334 E. 93rd Street 233-09-4555	25.____
26. GERALD MANN 16 LEXINGTON COURT 147-12-1612	Gerald Mann 16 Lexington Court 147-12-1216	26.____
27. ANN KELLEHER 354 GREENFIELD AVENUE 298-47-2316	Ann Kelleher 355 Greenfield Avenue 298-47-2316	27.____
28. GORDON CRAIG 1019 125TH STREET 883-23-0941	Gordon Craig 1019 135th Street 883-23-0941	28.____
29. LEONARD SWEET 217 WEST 72ND STREET 244-45-2311	Leonard Sweet 217 West 72nd Street 244-54-2311	29.____
30. SARAH FREIDLANDER 761 BENSONHURST AVENUE 551-12-2981	Sarah Freidlander 761 Bensonhurst Avenue 551-12-2981	30.____

KEY (CORRECT ANSWERS)

		ERROR IN LIST II
1.	A	
2.	B	29<u>6</u>8 Canada Blvd.
3.	B	286-49-<u>32</u>11
4.	A	
5.	B	Michel<u>e</u>
6.	A	
7.	B	867-<u>23</u>-7399
8.	B	2<u>76</u>-79-2388
9.	B	Kingsely
10.	B	178<u>1</u>-Deluth Avenue
11.	B	1<u>86</u>3 York Street S.W.
12.	B	11 Ma<u>r</u>genta Road
13.	B	67<u>8</u>-03-4992
14.	B	1429-8<u>1</u>-111th Street
15.	B	4711-Gran<u>d</u> Street
16.	B	Sch<u>a</u>ffer
17.	B	223-83-4<u>7</u>49
18.	A	
19.	A	
20.	B	4<u>12</u> Ryan Road
21.	B	Ja<u>n</u>es
22.	B	Str<u>u</u>thers
23.	A	
24.	B	429-7<u>3</u>-3337
25.	A	
26.	B	147-12-1<u>21</u>6
27.	A	
28.	B	1019 1<u>35</u>th Street
29.	B	244-<u>54</u>-2311
30.	A	

RECORD KEEPING
EXAMINATION SECTION
TEST 1

DIRECTIONS: Each question or incomplete statement is followed by several suggested answers or completions. Select the one that BEST answers the question or completes the statement. *PRINT THE LETTER OF THE CORRECT ANSWER IN THE SPACE AT THE RIGHT.*

Questions 1-7.

DIRECTIONS: In answering Questions 1 through 7, use the following master list. For each question, determine where the name would fit on the master list. Each answer choice indicates right before or after the name in the answer choice.

    Aaron, Jane
    Armstead, Brendan
    Bailey, Charles
    Dent, Ricardo
    Grant, Mark
    Mars, Justin
    Methieu, Justine
    Parker, Cathy
    Sampson, Suzy
    Thomas, Heather

1. Schmidt, William
   A. Right before Cathy Parker
   B. Right after Heather Thomas
   C. Right after Suzy Sampson
   D. Right before Ricardo Dent

2. Asanti, Kendall
   A. Right before Jane Aaron
   B. Right after Charles Bailey
   C. Right before Justine Methieu
   D. Right after Brendan Armstead

3. O'Brien, Daniel
   A. Right after Justine Methieu
   B. Right before Jane Aaron
   C. Right after Mark Grant
   D. Right before Suzy Sampson

4. Marrow, Alison
   A. Right before Cathy Parker
   B. Right before Justin Mars
   C. Right before Mark Grant
   D. Right after Heather Thomas

5. Grantt, Marissa
   A. Right before Mark Grant
   B. Right after Mark Grant
   C. Right after Justin Mars
   D. Right before Suzy Sampson

6. Thompson, Heath 6._____
   A. Right after Justin Mars B. Right before Suzy Sampson
   C. Right after Heather Thomas D. Right before Cathy Parker

DIRECTIONS: Before answering Question 7, add in all of the names from Questions 1 through 6. Then fit the name in alphabetical order based on the new list.

7. Francisco, Mildred 7._____
   A. Right before Mark Grant B. Right after Marissa Grantt
   C. Right before Alison Marrow D. Right after Kendall Asanti

Questions 8-10.

DIRECTIONS: In answering Questions 8 through 10, compare each pair of names and addresses. Indicate whether they are the same or different in any way.

8. William H. Pratt, J.D.   William H. Pratt, J.D. 8._____
   Attourney at Law   Attorney at Law
   A. No differences   B. 1 difference
   C. 2 differences   D. 3 differences

9. 1303 Theater Drive,; Apt. 3-B   1330 Theatre Drive,; Apt. 3-B 9._____
   A. No differences   B. 1 difference
   C. 2 differences   D. 3 differences

10. Petersdorff, Briana and Mary   Petersdorff, Briana and Mary 10._____
    A. No differences   B. 1 difference
    C. 2 differences   D. 3 differences

11. Which of the following words, if any, are misspelled? 11._____
    A. Affordable   B. Circumstansial
    C. Legalese   D. None of the above

Questions 12-13.

DIRECTIONS: Questions 12 and 13 are to be answered on the basis of the following table.

Standardized Test Results for High School Students in District #1230

	English	Math	Science	Reading
High School 1	21	22	15	18
High School 2	12	16	13	15
High School 3	16	18	21	17
High School 4	19	14	15	16

The scores for each high school in the district were averaged out and listed for each subject tested. Scores of 0-10 are significantly below College Readiness Standards. 11-15 are below College Readiness, 16-20 meet College Readiness, and 21-25 are above College Readiness.

12. If the high schools need to meet or exceed in at least half the categories in order to NOT be considered "at risk," which schools are considered "at risk"? 12.____
    A. High School 2
    B. High School 3
    C. High School 4
    D. Both A and C

13. What percentage of subjects did the district as a whole meet or exceed College Readiness standards? 13.____
    A. 25%
    B. 50%
    C. 75%
    D. 100%

Questions 14-15.

DIRECTIONS: Questions 14 and 15 are to be answered on the basis of the following information.

You have seven employees working as a part of your team: Austin, Emily, Jeremy, Christina, Martin, Harriet, and Steve. You have just sent an e-mail informing them that there will be a mandatory training session next week. To ensure that work still gets done, you are offering the training twice during the week: once on Tuesday and also on Thursday. This way half the employees will still be working while the other half attend the training. The only other issue is that Jeremy doesn't work on Tuesdays and Harriet doesn't work on Thursdays due to compressed work schedules.

14. Which of the following is a possible attendance roster for the first training session? 14.____
    A. Emily, Jeremy, Steve
    B. Steve, Christina, Harriet
    C. Harriet, Jeremy, Austin
    D. Steve, Martin, Jeremy

15. If Harriet, Christina, and Steve attend the training session on Tuesday, which of the following is a possible roster for Thursday's training session? 15.____
    A. Jeremy, Emily, and Austin
    B. Emily, Martin, and Harriet
    C. Austin, Christina, and Emily
    D. Jeremy, Emily, and Steve

Questions 16-20.

DIRECTIONS: In answering Questions 16 through 20, you will be given a word and will need to choose the answer choice that is MOST similar or different to the word.

16. Which word means the SAME as *annual*? 16.____
    A. Monthly
    B. Usually
    C. Yearly
    D. Constantly

17. Which word means the SAME as *effort*? 17.____
    A. Energy
    B. Equate
    C. Cherish
    D. Commence

18. Which word means the OPPOSITE of *forlorn*? 18.____
    A. Neglected
    B. Lethargy
    C. Optimistic
    D. Astonished

19. Which word means the SAME as *risk*? 19.____
    A. Admire
    B. Hazard
    C. Limit
    D. Hesitant

4 (#1)

20. Which word means the OPPOSITE of *translucent*? 20.____
    A. Opaque   B. Transparent   C. Luminous   D. Introverted

21. Last year, Jamie's annual salary was $50,000. Her boss called her today 21.____
    to inform her that she would receive a 20% raise for the upcoming year. How
    much more money will Jamie receive next year?
    A. $60,000   B. $10,000   C. $1,000   D. $51,000

22. You and a co-worker work for a temp hiring agency as part of their office 22.____
    staff. You both are given 6 days off per month. How many days off are you
    and your co-worker given in a year?
    A. 24   B. 72   C. 144   D. 48

23. If Margot makes $34,000 per year and she works 40 hours per week for 23.____
    all 52 weeks, what is her hourly rate?
    A. $16.34/hour   B. $17.00/hour   C. $15.54/hour   D. $13.23/hour

24. How many dimes are there in $175.00? 24.____
    A. 175   B. 1,750   C. 3,500   D. 17,500

25. If Janey is three times as old as Emily, and Emily is 3, how old is Janey? 25.____
    A. 6   B. 9   C. 12   D. 15

KEY (CORRECT ANSWERS)

1. C
2. D
3. A
4. B
5. B

6. C
7. A
8. B
9. C
10. A

11. B
12. A
13. D
14. B
15. A

16. C
17. A
18. C
19. B
20. A

21. B
22. C
23. A
24. B
25. B

TEST 2

DIRECTIONS: Each question or incomplete statement is followed by several suggested answers or completions. Select the one that BEST answers the question or completes the statement. *PRINT THE LETTER OF THE CORRECT ANSWER IN THE SPACE AT THE RIGHT.*

Questions 1-6.

DIRECTIONS: Questions 1 through 6 are to be answered on the basis of the following information.

item	name of item to be ordered
quantity	minimum number that can be ordered
beginning amount	amount in stock at start of month
amount received	amount receiving during month
ending amount	amount in stock at end of month
amount used	amount used during month
amount to order	will need at least as much of each item as used in the previous month
unit price	cost of each unit of an item
total price	total price for the order

Item	Quantity	Beginning	Received	Ending	Amount Used	Amount to Order	Unit Price	Total Price
Pens	10	22	10	8	24	20	$0.11	$2.20
Spiral notebooks	8	30	13	12			$0.25	
Binder clips	2 boxes	3 boxes	1 box	1 box			$1.79	
Sticky notes	3 packs	12 packs	4 packs	2 packs			$1.29	
Dry erase markers	1 pack (dozen)	34 markers	8 markers	40 markers			$16.49	
Ink cartridges (printer)	1 cartridge	3 cartridges	1 cartridge	2 cartridges			$79.99	
Folders	10 folders	25 folders	15 folders	10 folders			$1.08	

1. How many packs of sticky notes were used during the month?
   A. 16   B. 10   C. 12   D. 14

2. How many folders need to be ordered for next month?
   A. 15   B. 20   C. 30   D. 40

3. What is the total price of notebooks that you will need to order?
   A. $6.00   B. $0.25   C. $4.50   D. $2.75

4. Which of the following will you spend the second most money on?
   A. Ink cartridges   B. Dry erase markers
   C. Sticky notes   D. Binder clips

5. How many packs of dry erase markers should you order?
   A. 1   B. 8   C. 12   D. 0

6. What will be the total price of the file folders you order? 6.____
   A. $20.16   B. $21.60   C. $10.80   D. $4.32

Questions 7-11.

DIRECTIONS: Questions 7 through 11 are to be answered on the basis of the following table.

Number of Car Accidents, By Location and Cause, for 2014						
	Location 1		Location 2		Location 3	
Cause	Number	Percent	Number	Percent	Number	Percent
Severe Weather	10		25		30	
Excessive Speeding	20	40	5		10	
Impaired Driving	15		15	25	8	
Miscellaneous	5		15		2	4
TOTALS	50	100	60	100	50	100

7. Which of the following is the third highest cause of accidents for all three locations? 7.____
   A. Severe Weather
   B. Impaired Driving
   C. Miscellaneous
   D. Excessive Speeding

8. The average number of Severe Weather accidents per week at Location 3 for the year (52 weeks) was MOST NEARLY 8.____
   A. 0.57   B. 30   C. 1   D. 1.25

9. Which location had the LARGEST percentage of accidents caused by Impaired Driving? 9.____
   A. 1   B. 2   C. 3   D. Both A and B

10. If one-third of the accidents at all three locations resulted in at least one fatality, what is the LEAST amount of deaths caused by accidents last year? 10.____
    A. 60   B. 106   C. 66   D. 53

11. What is the percentage of accidents caused by miscellaneous means from all three locations in 2014? 11.____
    A. 5%   B. 10%   C. 13%   D. 25%

12. How many pairs of the following groups of letters are exactly alike? 12.____
    ACDOBJ   ACDBOJ
    HEWBWR   HEWRWB
    DEERVS   DEERVS
    BRFQSX   BRFQSX
    WEYRVB   WEYRVB
    SPQRZA   SQRPZA

    A. 2   B. 3   C. 4   D. 5

Questions 13-19.

DIRECTIONS: Questions 13 through 19 are to be answered on the basis of the following information.

In 2012, the most current information on the American population was finished. The information was compiled by 200 volunteers in each of the 50 states. The territory of Puerto Rico, a sovereign of the United States, had 25 people assigned to compile data. In February of 2010, volunteers in each state and sovereign began collecting information. In Puerto Rico, data collection finished by January 31st, 2011, while work in the United States was completed on June 30, 2012. Each volunteer gathered data on the population of their state or sovereign. When the information was compiled, volunteers sent reports to the nation's capital, Washington, D.C. Each volunteer worked 20 hours per month and put together 10 reports per month. After the data was compiled in total, 50 people reviewed the data and worked from January 2012 to December 2012.

13. How many reports were generated from February 2010 to April 2010 in Illinois and Ohio?
    A. 3,000   B. 6,000   C. 12,000   D. 15,000

14. How many volunteers in total collected population data in January 2012?
    A. 10,000   B. 2,000   C. 225   D. 200

15. How many reports were put together in May 2012?
    A. 2,000   B. 50,000   C. 100,000   D. 100,250

16. How many hours did the Puerto Rican volunteers work in the fall (September-November)?
    A. 60   B. 500   C. 1,500   D. 0

17. How many workers were compiling or reviewing data in July 2012?
    A. 25   B. 50   C. 200   D. 250

18. What was the total amount of hours worked by Nevada volunteers in July 2010?
    A. 500   B. 4,000   C. 4,500   D. 5,000

19. How many reviewers worked in January 2013?
    A. 75   B. 50   C. 0   D. 25

20. John has to file 10 documents per shelf. How many documents would it take for John to fill 40 shelves?
    A. 40   B. 400   C. 4,500   D. 5,000

21. Jill wants to travel from New York City to Los Angeles by bike, which is approximately 2,772 miles. How many miles per day would Jill need to average if she wanted to complete the trip in 4 weeks?
    A. 100   B. 89   C. 99   D. 94

4 (#2)

22. If there are 24 CPU's and only 7 monitors, how many more monitors do you need to have the same amount of monitors as CPU's?
    A. Not enough information
    B. 17
    C. 31
    D. 0

    22.____

23. If Gerry works 5 days a week and 8 hours each day, and John works 3 days a week and 10 hours each day, how many more hours per year will Gerry work than John?
    A. They work the same amount of hours.
    B. 450
    C. 520
    D. 832

    23.____

24. Jimmy gets transferred to a new office. The new office has 25 employees, but only 16 are there due to a blizzard. How many coworkers was Jimmy able to meet on his first day?
    A. 16   B. 25   C. 9   D. 7

    24.____

25. If you do a fundraiser for charities in your area and raise $500 total, how much would you give to each charity if you were donating equal amounts to 3 of them?
    A. $250.00   B. $167.77   C. $50.00   D. $111.11

    25.____

KEY (CORRECT ANSWERS)

1.	D		11.	C
2.	B		12.	B
3.	A		13.	C
4.	C		14.	A
5.	D		15.	C
6.	B		16.	C
7.	D		17.	B
8.	A		18.	B
9.	A		19.	C
10.	D		20.	B

21.	C
22.	B
23.	C
24.	A
25.	B

TEST 3

DIRECTIONS: Each question or incomplete statement is followed by several suggested answers or completions. Select the one that BEST answers the question or completes the statement. *PRINT THE LETTER OF THE CORRECT ANSWER IN THE SPACE AT THE RIGHT.*

Questions 1-3.

DIRECTIONS: In answering Questions 1 through 3, choose the correctly spelled word.

1. A. allusion B. alusion C. allusien D. allution 1.____

2. A. altitude B. alltitude C. atlitude D. altlitude 2.____

3. A. althogh B. allthough C. althrough D. although 3.____

Questions 4-9.

DIRECTIONS: In answering Questions 4 through 9, choose the answer that BEST completes the analogy.

4. Odometer is to mileage as compass is to 4.____
   A. speed B. needle C. hiking D. direction

5. Marathon is to race as hibernation is to 5.____
   A. winter B. dream C. sleep D. bear

6. Cup is to coffee as bowl is to 6.____
   A. dish B. spoon C. food D. soup

7. Flow is to river as stagnant is to 7.____
   A. pool B. rain C. stream D. canal

8. Paw is to cat as hoof is to 8.____
   A. lamb B. horse C. lion D. elephant

9. Architect is to building as sculptor is to 9.____
   A. museum B. chisel C. stone D. statue

Questions 10-14.

DIRECTIONS: Questions 10 through 14 are to be answered on the basis of the following graph.

Population of Carroll City Broken Down by Age and Gender (in Thousands)			
Age	Female	Male	Total
Under 15	60	60	120
15-23		22	
24-33		20	44
34-43	13	18	31
44-53	20		67
64 and Over	65	65	130
TOTAL	230	232	462

10. How many people in the city are between the ages of 15-23?
    A. 70   B. 46,000   C. 70,000   D. 225,000

11. Approximately what percentage of the total population of the city was female aged 24-33?
    A. 10%   B. 5%   C. 15%   D. 25%

12. If 33% of the males have a job and 55% of females don't have a job, which of the following statements is TRUE?
    A. Males have approximately 2,600 more jobs than females.
    B. Females have approximately 49,000 more jobs than males.
    C. Females have approximately 26,000 more jobs than males.
    D. None of the above statements are true.

13. How many females between the ages of 15-23 live in Carroll City?
    A. 67,000   B. 24,000   C. 48,000   D. 91,000

14. Assume all males 44-53 living in Carroll City are employed. If two-thirds of males age 44-53 work jobs outside of Carroll City, how many work within city limits?
    A. 31,333
    B. 15,667
    C. 47,000
    D. Cannot answer the question with the information provided

Questions 15-16.

DIRECTIONS: Questions 15 and 16 are labeled as shown. Alphabetize them for filing. Choose the answer that correctly shows the order.

15. (1) AED
    (2) OOS
    (3) FOA
    (4) DOM
    (5) COB

    A. 2-5-4-3-2   B. 1-4-5-2-3   C. 1-5-4-2-3   D. 1-5-4-3-2

16. Alphabetize the names of the people. Last names are given last.
    (1) Lindsey Jamestown
    (2) Jane Alberta
    (3) Ally Jamestown
    (4) Allison Johnston
    (5) Lyle Moreno

    A. 2-1-3-4-5   B. 3-4-2-1-5   C. 2-3-1-4-5   D. 4-3-2-1-5

17. Which of the following words is misspelled?
    A. disgust   B. whisper
    C. locale   D. none of the above

Questions 18-21.

DIRECTIONS: Questions 18 through 21 are to be answered on the basis of the following list of employees.

    Robertson, Aaron
    Bacon, Gina
    Jerimiah, Trace
    Gillette, Stanley
    Jacks, Sharon

18. Which employee name would come in third in alphabetized list?
    A. Robertson, Aaron   B. Jerimiah, Trace
    C. Gillette, Stanley   D. Jacks, Sharon

19. Which employee's first name starts with the letter in the alphabet that is five letters after the first letter of their last name?
    A. Jerimiah, Trace   B. Bacon, Gina
    C. Jacks, Sharon   D. Gillette, Stanley

20. How many employees have last names that are exactly five letters long?
    A. 1   B. 2   C. 3   D. 4

21. How many of the employees have either a first or last name that starts with the letter "G"?
    A. 1   B. 2   C. 4   D. 5

Questions 22-25.

DIRECTIONS: Questions 22 through 25 are to be answered on the basis of the following chart.

Bicycle Sales (Model #34JA32)							
Country	May	June	July	August	September	October	Total
Germany	34	47	45	54	56	60	296
Britain	40	44	36	47	47	46	260
Ireland	37	32	32	32	34	33	200
Portugal	14	14	14	16	17	14	89
Italy	29	29	28	31	29	31	177
Belgium	22	24	24	26	25	23	144
Total	176	198	179	206	208	207	1166

22. What percentage of the overall total was sold to the German importer?
    A. 25.3%   B. 22%   C. 24.1%   D. 23%

23. What percentage of the overall total was sold in September?
    A. 24.1%   B. 25.6%   C. 17.9%   D. 24.6%

24. What is the average number of units per month imported into Belgium over the first four months shown?
    A. 26   B. 20   C. 24   D. 31

25. If you look at the three smallest importers, what is their total import percentage?
    A. 35.1%   B. 37.1%   C. 40%   D. 28%

KEY (CORRECT ANSWERS)

1. A
2. A
3. D
4. D
5. C

6. D
7. A
8. B
9. D
10. C

11. B
12. C
13. C
14. B
15. D

16. C
17. D
18. D
19. B
20. B

21. B
22. A
23. C
24. C
25. A

TEST 4

DIRECTIONS: Each question or incomplete statement is followed by several suggested answers or completions. Select the one that BEST answers the question or completes the statement. *PRINT THE LETTER OF THE CORRECT ANSWER IN THE SPACE AT THE RIGHT.*

Questions 1-6.

DIRECTIONS: In answering Questions 1 through 6, choose the sentence that represents the BEST example of English grammar.

1. A. Joey and me want to go on a vacation next week.
   B. Gary told Jim he would need to take some time off.
   C. If turning six years old, Jim's uncle would teach Spanish to him.
   D. Fax a copy of your resume to Ms. Perez and me.

   1.____

2. A. Jerry stood in line for almost two hours.
   B. The reaction to my engagement was less exciting than I thought it would be.
   C. Carlos and me have done great work on this project.
   D. Two parts of the speech needs to be revised before tomorrow.

   2.____

3. A. Arriving home, the alarm was tripped.
   B. Jonny is regarded as a stand up guy, a responsible parent, and he doesn't give up until a task is finished.
   C. Each employee must submit a drug test each month.
   D. One of the documents was incinerated in the explosion.

   3.____

4. A. As soon as my parents get home, I told them I finished all of my chores.
   B. I asked my teacher to send me my missing work, check my absences, and how did I do on my test.
   C. Matt attempted to keep it concealed from Jenny and me.
   D. If Mary or him cannot get work done on time, I will have to split them up.

   4.____

5. A. Driving to work, the traffic report warned him of an accident on Highway 47.
   B. Jimmy has performed well this season.
   C. Since finishing her degree, several job offers have been given to Cam.
   D. Our boss is creating unstable conditions for we employees.

   5.____

6. A. The thief was described as a tall man with a wiry mustache weighing approximately 150 pounds.
   B. She gave Patrick and I some more time to finish our work.
   C. One of the books that he ordered was damaged in shipping.
   D. While talking on the rotary phone, the car Jim was driving skidded off the road.

   6.____

Questions 7-9.

DIRECTIONS: Questions 7 through 9 are to be answered on the basis of the following graph.

Ice Lake Frozen Flight (2002-2013)		
Year	Number of Participants	Temperature (Fahrenheit)
2002	22	4°
2003	50	33°
2004	69	18°
2005	104	22°
2006	108	24°
2007	288	33°
2008	173	9°
2009	598	39°
2010	698	26°
2011	696	30°
2012	777	28°
2013	578	32°

7. Which two year span had the LARGEST difference between temperatures?
   A. 2002 and 2003
   B. 2011 and 2012
   C. 2008 and 2009
   D. 2003 and 2004

8. How many total people participated in the years after the temperature reached at least 29°?
   A. 2,295   B. 1,717   C. 2,210   D. 4,543

9. In 2007, the event saw 288 participants, while in 2008 that number dropped to 173. Which of the following reasons BEST explains the drop in participants?
   A. The event had not been going on that long and people didn't know about it.
   B. The lake water wasn't cold enough to have people jump in.
   C. The temperature was too cold for many people who would have normally participated.
   D. None of the above reasons explain the drop in participants.

10. In the following list of numbers, how many times does 4 come just after 2 when 2 comes just after an odd number?
    23652476538986324885724863924244
    A. 2   B. 3   C. 4   D. 5

11. Which choice below lists the letter that is as far after B as S is after N in the alphabet?
    A. G   B. H   C. I   D. J

Questions 12-15.

DIRECTIONS: Questions 12 through 15 are to be answered on the basis of the following directory and list of changes.

Directory		
Name	Emp. Type	Position
Julie Taylor	Warehouse	Packer
James King	Office	Administrative Assistant
John Williams	Office	Salesperson
Ray Moore	Warehouse	Maintenance
Kathleen Byrne	Warehouse	Supervisor
Amy Jones	Office	Salesperson
Paul Jonas	Office	Salesperson
Lisa Wong	Warehouse	Loader
Eugene Lee	Office	Accountant
Bruce Lavine	Office	Manager
Adam Gates	Warehouse	Packer
Will Suter	Warehouse	Packer
Gary Lorper	Office	Accountant
Jon Adams	Office	Salesperson
Susannah Harper	Office	Salesperson

Directory Updates:
- Employee e-mail addresses will adhere to the following guidelines: lastnamefirstname@apexindustries.com (ex. Susannah Harper is harpersusannah@apexindustries.com). Currently, employees in the warehouse share one e-mail, distribution@apexindustries.com.
- The "Loader" position will now be referred to as "Specialist I"
- Adam Gates has accepted a Supervisor position within the Warehouse and is no longer a Packer. All warehouse employees report to the two Supervisors and all office employees report to the Manager.

12. Amy Jones tried to send an e-mail to Adam Gates, but it wouldn't send. Which of the following offers the BEST explanation?
    A. Amy put Adam's first name first and then his last name.
    B. Adam doesn't check his e-mail, so he wouldn't know if he received the e-mail or not.
    C. Adam does not have his own e-mail.
    D. Office employees are not allowed to send e-mails to each other.

13. How many Packers currently work for Apex Industries?
    A. 2   B. 3   C. 4   D. 5

14. What position does Lisa Wong currently hold?
    A. Specialist I
    B. Secretary
    C. Administrative Assistant
    D. Loader

15. If an employee wanted to contact the office manager, which of the following e-mails should the e-mail be sent to? 15.____
    A. officemanager@apexindustries.com
    B. brucelavine@apexindustries.com
    C. lavinebruce@apexindustries.com
    D. distribution@apexindustries.com

Questions 16-19.

DIRECTIONS: In answering Questions 16 through 19, compare the three names, numbers or addresses.

16. Smiley Yarnell   Smiley Yarnel   Smily Yarnell 16.____
    A. All three are exactly alike.
    B. The first and second are exactly alike.
    C. The second and third are exactly alike.
    D. All three are different.

17. 1583 Theater Drive   1583 Theater Drive   1583 Theatre Drive 17.____
    A. All three are exactly alike.
    B. The first and second are exactly alike.
    C. The second and third are exactly alike.
    D. All three are different.

18. 3341893212   3341893212   3341893212 18.____
    A. All three are exactly alike.
    B. The first and second are exactly alike.
    C. The second and third are exactly alike.
    D. All three are different.

19. Douglass Watkins   Douglas Watkins   Douglass Watkins 19.____
    A. All three are exactly alike.
    B. The first and third are exactly alike.
    C. The second and third are exactly alike.
    D. All three are different.

Questions 20-24.

DIRECTIONS: In answering Questions 20 through 24, you will be presented with a word. Choose the synonym that BEST represents the word in question.

20. Flexible 20.____
    A. delicate   B. inflammable   C. strong   D. pliable

21. Alternative 21.____
    A. choice   B. moderate   C. lazy   D. value

5 (#4)

22. Corroborate
    A. examine   B. explain   C. verify   D. explain   22.____

23. Respiration
    A. recovery   B. breathing   C. sweating   D. selfish   23.____

24. Negligent
    A. lazy   B. moderate   C. hopeless   D. lax   24.____

25. Plumber is to Wrench as Painter is to
    A. pipe   B. shop   C. hammer   D. brush   25.____

KEY (CORRECT ANSWERS)

1. D
2. A
3. D
4. C
5. B

6. C
7. C
8. B
9. C
10. C

11. A
12. C
13. A
14. A
15. C

16. D
17. B
18. A
19. B
20. D

21. A
22. C
23. B
24. D
25. D